People Are Talking

I've taken every sales course known to man. Chuck Blakeman's approach in Sell Less, Earn More is by far the best.

—ANDY CUNNINGHAM,
REAL ESTATE DEVELOPER

I implemented the tools in this book after a really rough year. I had my best year ever the next year, followed by my best year after that, and the next two years were consecutively each better than the year before. I always believed my business should produce more money in LESS time for me, and now every year it does.

—CAMERON MORGAN,
FINANCIAL ADVISOR, A&I WEALTH MANAGEMENT

The business growth approach Sell Less, Earn More is uniquely easy to implement, relentless in generating and closing potential Clients, and central in getting me off the sales treadmill. Tools like the First Domino, Leading and Lagging Indicators, and the Three C's have all generated Connections, Conversations, and Clients to help us double our revenue. I highly recommend this book.

—JUAN SANCHEZ,
CEO AND FOUNDER OF ZOOMINGMARKETS

I had hundreds of Clients as a result of chasing strangers before I learned the principles and practices in this book. Now I have just a few dozen Clients, and our revenue is exponentially higher because we don't focus on chasing strangers anymore, but on cultivating existing relationships.

—JASON DERINGER,
WEALTH MANAGER

When I first learned these Sell Less, Earn More principles and practices, I doubled my business in the eight weeks that followed, and in a few more weeks, I had quadrupled it.

—ELVI BJORG,
ELVI BJORG MARKETING

Using the Sell Less, Earn More principles and practices, I went from seeing myself as "self-employed" and working endlessly to building a real business that doesn't depend on me anymore to make it run. It's been a phenomenal, life-changing mindset shift for me.

—STACY VOGEL,
NORTH STAR, INC.

DOUBLE YOUR INCOME

in 90 Days with People You Already Know

SELL LESS EARN MORE

Chuck Blakeman

Entrepreneur Press®

Entrepreneur Press, Publisher
Cover Design: Mayfly Book Design
Production and Composition: Mike Fontecchio, Faith & Family Publications

Library of Congress Cataloging-in-Publication Data

Names: Blakeman, Chuck, author.

Title: Sell less, earn more : double your income in 90 days with people you already know / Chuck Blakeman.

Description: Irvine, CA : Entrepreneur Press, [2024] | Includes index. | Summary: "Instead of transactional encounters with strangers, learn how to double your income by deepening relationships with people you already know"-- Provided by publisher.

Identifiers: LCCN 2024036028 (print) | LCCN 2024036029 (ebook) | ISBN 9781642011814 (paperback) | ISBN 9781613084915 (epub)

Subjects: LCSH: Customer relations. | Customer services--Management. | Interpersonal relations. | Success in business.

Classification: LCC HF5415.5 .B525 2024 (print) | LCC HF5415.5 (ebook) | DDC 658.8/12--dc23/eng/20241203

LC record available at https://lccn.loc.gov/2024036028

LC ebook record available at https://lccn.loc.gov/2024036029

Table of Contents

*"You already know everyone you need to know
to make all your dreams come true."*

—BOB BEAUDINE,
BESTSELLING AUTHOR OF *THE POWER OF WHO*

*"To find people you have never met,
talk to people you already know."*

—CHUCK BLAKEMAN

Acknowledgments

A huge and eternal thanks to those who helped me learn so many of the principles I have used in business development for decades now, and taught who taught me some of the practices and tools themselves, which I would never have come to without their genius and their help.

Art Radtke developed the foundational ideas for some tools I still use and contributed greatly to my healthier understanding of business development.

Mort Murphy, Bill Davis, Meg Oltman, Jim Roman, and others helped develop and work on *Sell Less, Earn More* practices in early iterations of what we now call FasTrak, a business development course that teaches how to grow your Client base very quickly.

Early on, Arnell Tanyag facilitated FasTrak and taught some early iterations of the principles, practices, and tools in *Sell Less, Earn More*. We have built extensively on the foundation he laid.

Eddie Drescher, along with Arnell, myself, and others, experimented and helped refine and develop some of these early tools.

John Heenan, who introduced me to the above people and remains a good friend and sounding board, continues to faithfully practice these tools on the east side of the Atlantic.

Mark Bellestri, our Chief Dot Connector, inspires me with his dogged determination to get these tools in the hands of business owners all over the world by improving our systems, processes, approach, and presence.

Megan Kauffman, our Chief Results Officer, prevented all of us at the Crankset Group from running into brick walls for years, and always kept things humming.

Sandy Corrigan, our Chief Conation Officer, is a supportive friend, advocate, and connector for Crankset Group.

Thom Corrigan, our Chief 3to5 Club Facilitator, is also a great friend and is deeply passionate about helping other business owners live great, meaningful, and fulfilling lives.

Scott Connors, our Chief Change Officer, is out there on a daily basis, relentlessly and faithfully making it happen with bigger companies, transforming businesses and changing lives.

And Diane Blakeman, our Chief Relationship Officer and my chief advocate, spouse, and friend, provides stability for all of us crazies.

And especially to the many hundreds of FasTrakers on multiple continents who have taken FasTrak, the 90-day double your income challenge, over the past two decades, who still meet "live" with me and other 3to5 Club Facilitators online. You have taught me what really works on the ground and in the trenches, and from you I learned how to communicate those things simply and effectively. Thank you.

I trust the principles, tools, and practices we have all learned and developed together will help change the narrative around what it means to do business in a fast-moving world that needs a new operating system for finding and approaching potential Customers. And in the process, I trust we will see thousands of other business owners and Independent Agents permanently get off the sales treadmill.

Let's all continue to learn how to change the narrative: To *Sell Less, Earn More, let's commit to serve, not sell.*

RESULTS MAY VARY—
YOURS COULD BE BETTER

*I've taken every sales course known to man. The principles,
practices, and tools in Sell Less, Earn More are
not just unique—they are by far the best.*

—ANDY CUNNINGHAM,
INTERNATIONAL CORPORATE EXECUTIVE TURNED REAL ESTATE DEVELOPER

*Learn to be interested, not interesting. You'll sell a lot
more of everything—without having to sell it.*

—CHUCK BLAKEMAN

Selling is not natural. It had to be invented.

Most of what small business owners and Independent Agents
learned from the Industrial Age Factory System model of selling
is still in use, and it is still broken. And sales gurus are still trying
to get you to double down on the "tricks" and turn you into a slick
salesperson. But there's a better way.

The cold call, "stab you with my business card" approach
was already a bad idea back when the Factory System invented
salespeople, and it's an even worse idea in today's saturated marketing
world. So much of what is wrong with business (and not much that is

right) came from the legacy of these smoke-stacked 1900s pufferies spewing nonsense about:

- target markets (I'm not a "target," I'm Chuck.)
- selling to strangers (I buy from friends.)
- pitching (Do you even know what I need yet?)
- persuading (You're selling, which makes me not want to buy.)
- pain points (I buy from my joy points.)
- uninvited ongoing contact (aka stalking)
- emotional manipulation (narcissism)
- controlling the conversation (I want to be heard.)
- cold calls (I choose my friends.)
- "closing" the sale (I'll buy if I want to, not from pressure.)
- the sale is the goal (*Serving* by adding value is the goal.)
- false scarcity (Your scarcity scares me; I live in abundance.)
- "I contacted my database" (Really? What if you just "connected with somebody you know"?)

Even the word "sales" is broken. It has become so closely identified with things we don't like that the term "business development," which was traditionally about finding future markets, has instead on becoming a synonym for sales (a present activity, not a future one). I use it now, too, because the term "salesperson" is now like a sign on a box reading "Caution: Sharp Objects Inside."

Who Needs Another Sales Book?

If you're a business owner, Independent Agent, or reluctant salesperson who doesn't light up at the prospect of stabbing strangers with your business card, then you do—and so do I. There's nothing new in this book, but any author selling you that line is either being disingenuous or indulging in wishful thinking. As I said in my first book, *Making Money Is Killing Your Business*,[1] I've never had an original thought in my life, but I'm OK with that, because I'm pretty sure you haven't either. The wisdom is all out there by now, and the best we can hope for is to rediscover something we've ignored and repackage it in a way that is fresh, relevant, and newly meaningful. I trust this book will be that for you.

This book is a reminder of beautiful and essential relational principles and practices we lost when we moved from building things in homes and shops to the Industrial Age Factory System of the 1800s. The Factory System gave us great toys and amazing technology, but dehumanized everything about work and how we approach one another when we're there.

And it unfortunately invented salespeople. Nothing at work is in need of more rehumanizing than how we view and connect with potential Customers and Clients. And as we reacquaint ourselves with these lost principles and practices of humanity, they will improve every relationship you have because Clients are people, too. And the sooner we start treating them like people again, the more they will love and buy from us.

Sell Less, Earn More isn't about convincing you that aggressively stabbing people with your business card, if you even still have one, is not helpful. We're way past that. This is a book about how to live out the principles of relationship-focused business on the ground and in the trenches, with practices I have learned and used myself over many decades—without becoming a salesperson.

The principles, practices, and tools you learn in this book will result in a Steady Stream of Potential Clients, not just leads, and they work regardless of your industry or profession and whether you sell services or products. This book will help you adopt a few seemingly new yet really pre-Industrial Age sales practices, and you'll see your top-line revenue go up fast as a result. We're not going "back to the

---

1   Published as the number one business book of the year in 2010 and soon to be released in a freshly revised and updated version under a new title, *The Purpose-Driven Business*.

future"; as it turns out, our sales future lies behind us, in the time before we invented smokestacks.

The Cure for the Common Cold Call: In order to *sell less and earn more, we need to commit to* serving, not selling.

We want to help you readopt the long-lost, preindustrial customer interaction principle many owners used for centuries in shops and home businesses; "serve; don't sell." If you use this simple principle, you can sell less and earn more, and potentially see your business explode (there's no silver bullet guarantee; that's what you get from the slick salesperson). Contrary to what business schools have taught for more than a century, great business is relational first, and transactional only very secondarily. Putting other people's needs above your need to sell is central to being even more successful than you are now.

Most sales processes are stuck in the Factory System, trying to get you to "transact." What if instead, you knew what people needed and got them *that*, even if it meant not selling them your product or service? Really? Yes, really. You're about to find out what a treasure the principle "serve; don't sell" has been for me to figure out how to sell less and earn more, and I trust it will be equally useful for you going forward.

In *Sell Less, Earn More*, we'll take a different but proven direction in sales that was around long before the Factory System ever caused us to lose our way. I truly believe that if you never talked about your business again, unless somebody asked first, that you would close more sales and make more money. To paraphrase a well-known anonymous quote, "Culture eats strategy for lunch," we'll add,

Serving eats selling for breakfast.

You're a Snowflake, Not a Flake

Unique is not wrong, it's normal. Every one of us is unique. And unlike most sales process books, this one doesn't require everyone to follow the same rigid process, "proven" to work by the guru. This book presents principles, practices, and tools you can *choose from* to fit your personality and unique way of showing up in life and business.

"One-size-fits-all" sales processes should be a yellow warning flag. The best business development people (remember, that's code for sales now) don't rigidly follow processes developed by a guru for the masses. They find things that work well for them and flourish because of it. We've had people double their income in a few months by adopting just one of the practices we share. This book will help you find the few tools that uniquely work for you because they make bringing on new Clients an energizing experience instead of the drudgery of "sales" that has worn you down.

This book is for two distinct sets of businesspeople; the first is business owners, and the second is Independent Agents who have autonomy over their sales process, such as resellers, insurers, wealth managers, online influencers, real estate agents, and distributors. If you have the authority to design and control your own sales process, this book might become your sales bible. If you work for a manager who thinks they know the *only* way to sell is to hunt more strangers, this book will only frustrate you. Give it to your manager to read instead and see if the light goes on for them. Or maybe take the leap and go out on your own...

The 800-Pound Gorilla in the
Sales Training Room

Most sales training focuses on using databases, reading body language, building a website, using industry-appropriate colors, using the right phrases, leading people to "yes," and closing the sale. That's all good and necessary stuff. I built and ran three marketing support companies that helped people with those things, but the 800-pound gorilla in the room is this: Sales almost never break down because you chose the wrong word or made a lousy website. It breaks down because you don't have anyone to talk to. This book will show you what I learned: The key to bringing on a lot of new Customers or Clients quickly is not learning how to look good or close the sale, but having a *Steady Stream of Potential Clients*.

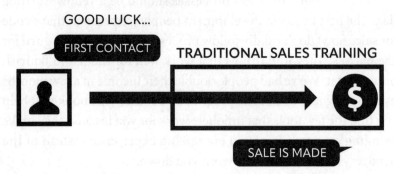

Figure F.1: The Traditional Sales Training Model

You can be the best salesperson/business developer in the world, but if you don't have anybody to talk to, you're going to go hungry. The opposite is not true. You can be a lousy salesperson, but if you have a steady stream of people to talk to, you're going to bring on some new Customers. And in the process, you'll learn how to be good at it—not because you trained in how to talk to people, but because you actually talked to people. Planning doesn't create movement. Movement creates the plan.

Double Your Income in 90 Days?
Many Have Done It

As I suggested above, results will vary, but yours will likely be much better if you go all in with the principle *Sell Less, Earn More* approach that is central to getting the result: *Sell Less, Earn More*. Almost all of us already do something to build relationships, so let's expand on that. Throughout this book, you'll read about real people who doubled their income, and sometimes their revenue, by using these tools and practices that have worked for me for a very long time because they went all in and left their old sales operating system behind.

I doubled my income the first time I applied these tools and principles and doubled it again a few years later (I don't ask anybody to do things I haven't done). A near-majority of people who have applied these things doubled their income in 90 days and a healthy majority achieved that goal within six months to a year. Many who didn't double their income still saw significant increases. And the ones who saw no impact, with a few understandable exceptions, read the material but didn't practice it for a full 90 days or more. We get what we intend, not what we hope for.

So stick with these tools for at least 90 days, and intend for something outrageous to happen. Don't just hope things will change. As the old saying that Art Radtke, a business advisor and an icon of small business advocates introduced me to many years ago says, "If you want something to change, you have to change something." Duh—and yet, not. Profound.

You get what you intend. Not what you hope for.

What do you intend to change in 90 days—or in the next six months or year? Come up with a measurable goal with a clear deadline that is at least slightly scary but doable if you work hard. What specifically do you want to double in the next 90 days? Your income? Just your disposable income? Your business revenue? Pick something challenging and go after it with intention.

And start with this mindset shift: serve; don't sell. This is the central principle of Sell Less, Earn More, and it affects every facet of our lives.

The Roller Coaster Treadmill of Business

Part of our objective here is to get off the Roller Coaster Treadmill of business, which starts with getting off the sales treadmill. You can fill the peaks and valleys of Figure F.2, below, with many different binary statements over 30 years: "I don't have enough Clients/I have too many Clients," "I don't have enough office space/I have too much space," "I don't have enough people/I have too many people," "I don't have enough production capacity/I have too much capacity," and even "I don't have enough money/I have too much money" (once the tax person cometh for their share). And after 30 years of being yanked around by this nonsense, you stop taking distributions for a year or so, create a false profit, and sell this mess to some other fool who will do it all over again for another 30 years. Welcome to business?

WHAT 30 YEARS OF BUSINESS LOOKS LIKE TOO OFTEN

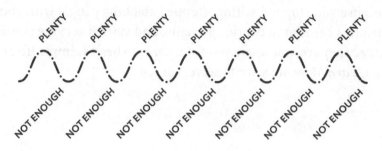

Figure F.2: The Roller Coaster Treadmill

The principles, practices, and tools that follow should help you level out the journey and make it much more reliable and sustainable—and a lot more rewarding (see Figure F.3 below). Let's figure out how to take the extremes out of business and especially out of sales. Let's make business more predictable.

What if you knew with Utter Clarity that if you just did one specific activity every week, you would acquire all the Customers you need to build the business you want? In Chapter 5, we'll show you how to do that by identifying what we call your First Domino, the most important number in your business. Bar none.

LEVEL OUT THE JOURNEY

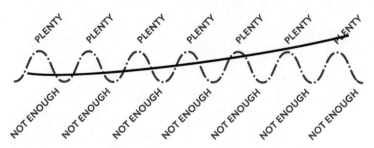

Figure F.3: A Steady Stream of Potential Clients

So embrace this new approach to relationship marketing, and I believe you will see your business take off. It will happen precisely because you stopped selling, stopped stabbing people with your business cards at networking events, and started serving people where they are, not where you want them to be. It's simple. To *Sell Less, Earn More,* we learn to serve, not sell.

Chapter 1

WHY DO WE SELL
TO STRANGERS?

*For 20 years I was a successful wealth manager, yet when I
implemented the Sell Less, Earn More system, my income doubled
almost right away. In the next few years using Sell Less, Earn More
system, I have gone from 2,200 Clients to less than 30 Clients, and
my personal income is more than 10 times what it was back then.*

—Jason Deringer

The closer you get to a hug, the more likely you are to sell something.

—Chuck Blakeman

We've been led astray by the still-prevalent Factory System approach to sales. The biggest problem in sales happens not when we're with a customer, but long before we ever meet them. We've been taught we need to control the conversation, be nice, respond to objections, read body language, find pain points, and learn the art of the close. But the biggest problem in sales for everyone is that we either don't have the right people to talk to, or more often, *anyone* to talk to. We don't need to know how to talk to potential customers until we have a steady stream of them wanting to meet with us.

A Steady Stream of Potential Clients

I'm not a natural-born salesperson. I was never the guy who could sell bathing suits at a ski resort. I have succeeded in my 13 businesses not because I was great at making sales, but because I learned how to develop a Steady Stream of Potential Clients. I don't mean a steady stream of strangers, but a steady stream of people who already know and like me, even if *they have never met me*, which happens often. How do we get to that place? We need to solve this one obstacle and create that steady stream, or nothing else matters. If you can learn how to get people to like you before they've even met you, you're going to have a great run. And you can, without being an influencer, writer, speaker, or social media maven. We all can. It's actually not that hard. We'll show you how on every page of this book.

RELATE OR TRANSACT?

To get there, we might need a mindset shift from what we've been taught about how to do sales for the past 150 years, which is to hunt strangers. We need a mindset that worked much better 250 years ago and will work much better today: building relationships in unique ways and then selling to people we already know. This works for everything from brick-and-mortar to online stores. Business development for business owners and Independent Agents should be more like talking with your neighbor at a barbecue, not a stranger across a desk; it should be a *relational* experience, not a *transactional* one. We are all better off when we move from selling to bringing awareness, from being the Persuader to being the Engager, who takes people as far as *they* want to go and then meets *their* needs, not our own.

Since the advent of the Industrial Age Factory System, business has been lost in a transactional vortex. The principal purpose of business has become to sell and service the product, not serve the customer. We've been led to believe that the fact people are affected by the process is largely an inconvenience or incidental to the true motivation behind all business, which Adam Smith famously and erroneously postulated in the 18th century: *self-interest*.[2] While self-interest may still be motivating most companies today, this author has experienced that this transactional view of business is actually at the root of people's disdain for how businesses focus on making money at the expense of the world around them. On the contrary, businesses who reject self-interest as their motivation and embrace the interest of their customers and the world around them perform better consistently, by every measure of business success.

In his book, **Re-Humanizing the Workplace (By Giving Everybody Their Brain Back),** *Chuck Blakeman studies top performing companies committed to serving, and not to self-interest, and shows how they perform at the top of their industries in every respect.*

Great companies know better, but most companies are still operating as if they exist in a Smithian transactional vacuum designed specifically to suck profits away from the rest of humanity. It's changing, but slowly. Which is a shame, because the data shows emphatically that when you're kind to people and treat them like adults, you make more money. Change is hard, and we rarely let the facts get in the way of our unhelpful emotional attachments to short-term, lizard-brain survival tactics like Industrial-Age self-interest. But there is a better way.

---

2   It's not coincidental that Adam Smith came up with his revision of capitalism, from serving others to self-interest, just when we started building factories, which changed the landscape of sales from building relationships to transacting "at" people. Smith was an industrialist, not a capitalist, a product of the Factory System that was built on extracting value, not adding it.

HOW SHOULD WE BUILD RELATIONSHIPS?

Pat walks into the bar, sees a woman by herself, walks up and introduces himself, and asks her name.

"My name is Jenna," she says.

Pat responds, "Great, Jenna, will you marry me?" (If Jenna says yes, they deserve each other.)

Relationships matter more than anything else in business, and cultivating them is the most important skill you will learn in order to gain new Clients or Customers and build a successful, vibrant, meaningful business. And you will get there faster with proven tools to help you, not just theories or principles.

Just about everything we've been taught in sales (and in business) for the past 175 years has supplanted thousands of years of doing business relationally with friends. Now we're taught to be transactional with strangers, which is counterproductive to making a sale. Great salespeople intuitively ignore the aggressive, in-your-face techniques they've been taught—and regularly get in trouble for it with their sales manager.

THE POWER OF RELATIONSHIPS

I worked as a captive employee twice, and during one of those experiences, the sales director flew into Denver to take me to lunch. She informed me that other members of the sales team were not happy because I was regularly out of the office, sometimes for multiple hours, and sometimes multiple times per week. And I never made the requisite 20-plus cold calls a week. In fact, I never made any, (and never have). She wanted me to get on the bandwagon, get in line, and start working the phone.

Fortunately, for once I was prepared. "Donna (not her real name), what result do you want from me?" Based on the quizzical look on her face, this question was unexpected, so I elaborated. "At the end of the year, what measure of success could I achieve that would make you and the company thrilled to have me working here?"

She knew where I was going. "Chuck, I understand you're already the leading salesperson in the company, and we appreciate that," she said. "But I need you to follow the process."

I responded, "Donna, I think it's important to remind you that our division has $13 million in sales, and I generated $7 million of that. The other six salespeople have all done $1 million each in sales this year following the company's process." "I realize that," she cut in, "but they're all doing 40-plus cold calls a week. You don't make any. Imagine where you could be if you did cold calls, too." (Yeah, it was a softball, so I took a swing.) "Donna, I'd be right where they are, generating $1 million a year in sales instead of $7 million," I said. "Is that the result you want at the end of the year, or would you like me to train them to do what I do instead?"

It's the rare sales director who would say yes, and she didn't either. It's understandable, because it's much easier to demonstrate your worth as a sales manager when you can turn in weekly reports showing you "motivated" seven salespeople to make a total of 280 cold calls to potential Clients. That's very flashy, and easily perceived as "productivity." And it's all very easily tied to the manager's pressure on them. It's a lot murkier to turn in a report that says, "Well, Chuck played golf with two people in the middle of the day this week and had lunch with two others, so he made four contacts. Except he wasn't even with potential Customers. He was with friends he already knows really well who probably won't ever buy anything from us. I'm not sure he's cut out for sales. I just can't get him to do sales things."

Despite having never made a cold call, I was the leading salesperson at two companies. In the second one, I wasn't even in sales—I was a marketing VP. When you take the time to carefully and respectfully build relationships and stay in touch, someone just might remember you helped them before and call you. You'll likely have a Steady Stream of Potential Clients without talking to strangers. And you can marry someone you know well, instead of a stranger at a bar. (Life's principles work everywhere, or they don't work at all.)

FRIENDS DON'T LET FRIENDS SELL TO FRIENDS

Jason owns his own company and functions as the primary salesperson, a good role for owners in early-stage companies. Jason shares, "I was told by everyone from my mother to multiple sales managers, 'Don't sell to your friends.'" When I finally figured out that all the people who already knew me were my greatest potential opportunity and got over the head trash that friendship and business just don't mix, everything changed. My closing rate skyrocketed, and now I spend a lot less time in sales and enjoy my business a lot more."

John Heenan, my dear friend in Belfast, Ireland, who built a very successful 3PL fulfillment company and also runs 3to5 Clubs for business owners in Ireland,[3] has a simple business principle. "When I meet with a potential Client, I ask myself, 'Would I want to take this person home to dinner with my family?'" he says. "If the answer is no, I'm not looking to do business with them." What a great, simple litmus test for the importance of prioritizing relationships over transactions, both in business and in life.

WHY ARE WE MORE COMFORTABLE SELLING TO STRANGERS?

Amber is in our FasTrak business development course as I'm writing this book. During her check-in with the group, she shared that she had connected with an existing Client who had committed to a significant increase in revenue spend with her. She wasn't sure if that "counted": "All I did was talk to someone I already know and asked them how I could serve them. It just feels a little bit like cheating because I didn't go find a new Client. I just talked very intentionally with someone I already knew." Our desire for this book is that we all learn that it's not cheating. In fact, that's the best sales strategy you can employ. And it will lead to bringing on Clients you didn't know, too.

---

3   For more on 3to5Clubs, visit 3to5Club.com.

We weren't always uncomfortable selling to friends. In fact, for the thousands of years that people have bought and sold things, they did so almost exclusively with people they knew as both neighbors and Customers. The notion of buying from strangers would have been greeted with suspicion. How do I know I can trust you? Who can vouch for you? Why haven't any of my friends bought from you yet? Will you be around if something goes wrong after I buy?

The Industrial Age Factory System is once again the culprit.[4] Before factories, we bought and sold with people we "knew, liked, and trusted," per Dale Carnegie. And the fact that he had to write a book to bring that idea back speaks volumes about the artificial, non-relational territory the world wandered into when the Factory System took over sales. Dale didn't quite get through. We used his ideas to put a shiny new coat of paint over the old one, but the building remained the same.

Creating Needs That Didn't Exist

As factories began to manufacture more products than we needed and then products we didn't know we needed, pestering people aggressively on sidewalks and in the town square became a normal way of dumping the excess production. Door-to-door intrusion—I mean sales—was very effective early on. In 1886, David McConnell started peddling his Avon perfumes door-to-door, and in 1910, the U.S. Direct Selling Association was formed, and your front door was never the same again. In the heyday of invading people's privacy in the 1950s and '60s, tens of thousands of people made a living selling door-to-door. Most sources say it's a tenth of that today, and one-third of today's door bangers work for giant corporations.

---

4   See my books *Why Employees Are Always a Bad Idea* (2014) and *Re-Humanizing the Workplace (By Giving Everybody Their Brain Back)* (2020).

About 60 percent of them quit within a year, because aggressive sales techniques don't work anymore. And they weren't a good idea when they did work, but people still do it.

When salesy types wore out their welcome on your front door mat, they discovered the phone. No more walking neighborhoods, no more brooms in the face, and much more efficient. We all know how much we love getting phone calls from strangers trying to sell us some life-changing product. (One guy calls me all the time, a Mr. Scam Likely. The dude is relentless.)

Now we've found a myriad of new ways to annoy strangers with our goods, a lot of it currently swirling around the internet. Seth Godin (author of *Permission Marketing: Turning Strangers into Friends and Friends into Customers*) made a justifiably big splash in the late 1990s by reintroducing a long-lost idea when he suggested we would make a lot more money if we stopped intruding on people's lives and only talked to them when we already had their permission. Duh. And, sadly, not duh. The shoe cobblers from 1725 would be proud of him, and we're all glad people like him have tried to right the sales ship. But the ship is still listing badly, and salespeople are still aggressively hunting down strangers and stabbing them with business cards.

What Is Marketing?

The year 1850 was the first time more things were made in a factory than in homes and shops, and by the 1880s, factories were producing more of almost everything than we could possibly consume. The new strategy required to solve this problem was called "marketing," a meaning of the word that first appeared in dictionaries in 1897 and wasn't studied in universities until the 20th century—another desperate invention of the Factory System.

I have owned multiple companies in the marketing space. It was not created to help us see value or expose us to things we needed. Advertising could do that and had been for centuries. The sign hanging outside a shop got you to come in, and it was up to the shopkeeper to explain the product to you. Marketing was invented to persuade us to buy things we don't need. It can be really helpful, but you should avoid using it how it was first intended, to sell things people don't need.

I mention marketing because small business owners have sadly learned from giant corporations, and the books written by people who run marketing for giant corporations, that marketing is separate from sales. It probably is for them, but it shouldn't be for small businesses. We shouldn't learn how to market from giant corporations any more than an antelope should learn how to eat from a *Tyrannosaurus rex*.

One of the major fallacies of business is that they all operate under the same rules. But giant corporations are akin to classical physics, which exists on a "visual" level, where small business is like quantum physics, which takes place on the subatomic level. They are so different that not only do the same rules not apply to both kinds of physics (or big and small businesses), but you can't even ask the same questions and expect to get a good answer.

For small business owners and independent business development people, marketing should only be thought of as two things:

1. **Indirect Sales.** Always think of your marketing as "indirect sales," also known as ROI, or Return on Investment Marketing. If you put a dollar into marketing, you want to get three or four dollars back, or even more to break even. If you're spending marketing money and can't *very* easily track it right back to sales, you're fooling yourself that it's working. Too often you're just doing ego marketing, or what the giant corporations get to call "brand recognition marketing."

Brand recognition marketing is OK for giant corporations, which can't meet with people and get to know them. It's an obscenely expensive and much less effective way to build a relationship. But it's all they've got. Please do not mimic them and spend a bunch of money trying to look good with fancy color palettes, subliminal designer website tricks, expensive logos, beautiful ads, focus groups, and other tricks of the trade. That kind of marketing is the biggest waste of money you will ever incur in your small business, because unlike the giants, you can't spend enough money to make it work.

As a small business, your brand is what people think, and, more important, feel, when they hear your name or the name of your business. Deliver a great product or service, and do it relationally, and you will have all the brand recognition marketing you will ever need. Once you reach multiple millions a year in sales, then you can start thinking about brand recognition marketing as the giants do it. Until then, build relationships and expect to get a very trackable return on any marketing you do.

Note: Some small companies do need to concern themselves with brand recognition marketing, but it's rare, and it's mostly in the consumer product space (cosmetics, foods, and some others). We'll use "Indirect" throughout this book to refer to marketing, to remind you of the only good use of marketing for most small businesses.

2. **Noise.** All marketing (both ROI and brand recognition) is just noise—nothing more, nothing less. The three questions around this noise are what matter:
   a. Is your noise louder than the other person's noise?
   b. If people hear it, is it attractional? Do people *want* to hear and lean into it, or away from it?
   c) If they hear it, does it sound like somebody else's noise, or is your noise unique?

It's very difficult to throw enough money at traditional marketing noise to make it "audible." Fortunately, there is a way to do marketing with almost no money involved.

The Four Quadrants of Marketing

So how do you find Customers now? How are you currently selling? Are you doing networking, cold calling, buying lists for email or direct mail advertising, personal referrals, TV, radio, newspapers, social media, blogging, podcasting, speaking?

I built and owned a couple of marketing support services companies from the ground up. From 1992 to 2006, I worked closely with advertising, branding, and marketing agencies. I learned a lot during those 14 years that validated work my acquaintance Art Radtke did in the early 2000s. I've continued to morph and twist his ideas around what I call the Four Quadrants of Marketing (see Figure 1.1 below).

Figure 1.1: The Four Quadrants of Marketing

The upper left quadrant is advertising, or what we refer to affectionately as the shotgun method. It's for giant corporations, not you (with rare exceptions—and no, you're probably not that exception). Advertising just blasts a message out randomly and hopes it hits the right person or company, who is actually interested when they get your ad. It works, but it is very high cost. And yet relationally it is also very low maintenance. McDonald's doesn't talk to anyone in their neighborhood, they just saturate your life with ads. Coca-Cola created more than 1 billion (with a B) impressions in 2016 with just one ad campaign. And you really think a $5,000 Google ad for just one month can compete with that?

Your ad gets buried every day by these behemoths. Don't even think about shotgun advertising until you have six or seven figures you can spend for *well* over a year, and then it still might not be enough to compete with the noise of giant corporations. It seems appealing to smaller businesses because you just throw money at the market and then wait for your phone to ring. But your noise will never cut through to get you the ROI you hoped for.

The lower left quadrant is direct marketing, which is more like a rifle than a shotgun, using whatever media can connect you "directly" to your potential customer (social media, text, email, or snail mail). It's much less expensive than advertising, but still a lot more than the quadrants on the right. Like advertising, it is reactive and also fairly low in actual human contact. Small businesses can use this quadrant very successfully, but it could also be an expensive experiment with very little return. In most cases, you need a professional to help you here, which adds to the cost. And unfortunately, direct marketing on the internet is still the Wild West, with many inexperienced, well-intentioned, but unhelpful marketers for every one who might actually bring you a good ROI.

The top right quadrant is public relations, which can be everything from very expensive to actually profitable—while still building a customer base. I knew one guy who wanted to build a website to sign up amateur rugby players for rugby tourism—bring your spouse to a rugby-crazed country for 10 to 14 days. He would have a couple of amateur games set up for them to play with the locals and a couple more to watch at the pro level. We suggested for his PR campaign, he spend a summer kicking a rugby ball across America, and with hotel, clothing, equipment, nutrition, and drink endorsements. Had he gone with our suggestion, he could have made a handsome profit while getting on the local news in every town and city he went through. Sometimes PR can also be paid marketing.

And sometimes PR is just an inexpensive gold mine. A few decades ago, a local dry cleaners in my city started a coat donation drive for people who couldn't afford one. Every year now, they get hundreds of thousands of dollars in free advertising from TV and other media, covering what has rightly become a big charity drive each year. Thousands of people get legitimate warm fuzzies every year for this company. Genius. And very low-cost ROI.

How can you make a splash, turn some heads, do some good, or be weird enough to get the media to cover you? We have a podcast sponsored by companies trying to reach our Clients. Social media influencers have learned this quadrant well. You can, too. And you might even get paid to do it.

THE SMALL BUSINESS MARKETING QUADRANT: RELATIONSHIPS

The lower right quadrant of marketing is about building relationships, one at a time or, better yet, by finding one person who can introduce you to a hundred of their best friends. It's very low-cost financially, but it will cost you in time: many 45-minute cups of coffee a year and lots of texts or phone calls to people you already know. But it is the best way for small businesses, and perhaps the only way for some, to get your first few orders or to break into new markets.

In a small business, you don't "have to" build relationships, you "get to." It's a lot more fun, especially for the introvert who isn't a fan of big events and prefers a quiet cup of coffee with a friend. It takes time and energy, but not very much money. And which of those do small businesses have more of? We don't have much of either, but frankly, when starting out, we have more time than money. We can't throw enough money at the market to create enough noise, but that's OK. You will discover later that the relationships you build early on will stick with you and come back to you in abundance. Investing in people is always worth the time.

All four of these quadrants will build relationships, but relationship marketing does it the fastest and the best for small businesses and Independent Agents. There's a simple maxim that has worked again and again for me:

The closer you get to a hug, the more likely you are to sell something.

TV is a long way from a hug, a direct mail piece is a tiny bit closer, and a phone call is even closer. But until you have that giant noisy advertising budget, sitting in the same room with someone will always be the best way to get a hug—and a Client.

One of the major lessons of quantum business is this: The smaller your business is, the more you need to live in the right-hand quadrants and the more you can beat the giants by simply building relationships in the lower right quadrant. Don't be fooled, your $100,000 in advertising will be swallowed whole by the whales.

Over and over, research has shown that no matter what business you're in or where it is focused (online or brick-and-mortar), the overwhelming majority of your future Clients will come from people you already know. So why focus on spending money to attract strangers? Instead, figure out how to regularly get your friends to bring you a Steady Stream of Potential Clients. This is the cure for the common cold call and a huge reduction in spend, and it's a lot more rewarding both financially and relationally. Let's get after it.

The Single Purpose of All Good Marketing—Building Relationships

Having built a few companies in the marketing space and worked with many others over several decades, I can confidently say that the only purpose of *good* marketing is to build relationships. Giant insurance companies don't sell insurance. They try to get you to love their goofy mascot or awkwardly funny spokesperson. Great online influences don't hawk their products, they relentlessly put out content that helps you get to know and like them.

You can spot bad marketing because it doesn't honor the need to build a relationship and get you to a hug, virtually or IRL. Instead, the vendor is hawking features, benefits, and persuasive sales stories with urgent closes. They're not even attempting to build a trusting relationship because they know you're not likely to buy from them again anyway. The lesson for us is to stop selling "at" people and figure out how to get them to want to buy. Serve; don't sell.

How to Build (Any) Business Relationships

After 35 years in business, I have found there are two keys to creating and nurturing relationships: *Recency* and *Frequency* (R&F). How recently have I talked to you, and how frequently do I talk to you? The guy who asked Jenna to marry him when they first met in the bar was "recent," but he hadn't been frequent. Jenna should run. And if you met with your best friend weekly for years and then stopped, the relationship is going to fade. Any healthy relationship requires ongoing Recency and Frequency.

It's no different in business, because we know intuitively that people in business are not "targets," "demographics," "contacts," or "users." They are people. And people buy from other people, not from companies. This R&F duality will stay with us through the rest of this book and, I trust, through the rest of your life and in every area of your life. Even your dog will appreciate it.

What R&F imply is that you can't just do a one-shot "will you marry me?" advertising campaign and expect someone to come be your friend. It was recent, but it wasn't frequent enough and therefore can lack trust, which is built over time through consistent, beneficial behavior. And you can't do a podcast for two years, stop, and think you've done it long enough. It was frequent, but now it's no longer recent. In Chapter 13, we'll talk about how to build a Drip System using R&F to help create your Steady Stream of Potential Clients without investing a lot of time and money into building or running it.

If R&F are the hallmarks of great marketing and great relationships, just *how* recently and frequently should I connect with you? One warning. For those of you who are overly aggressive (and if you're worried about it, you probably aren't), Recency and Frequency are also the tools of the stalker. Don't be a stalker. The rest of this book will give you tools and practices that are invitational and attractional. They will make people want to click on your invites or walk toward you when they see you coming. For some it will be a big mindset shift, while for others, it's just permission to do what you intuitively have always known made sense: make friends with very intentional practices.

My Next One Thing: Relationship Marketing

List the ways you are currently selling and connect them with one or more of the four marketing quadrants above that you think they belong in. For a small business owner, the vast majority of them should be relational, even if your business is online. The most successful online sites were promoted by people who knew, liked, and trusted their owners. The same is true for brick-and-mortar businesses.

Current marketing and selling methods:

_____

_____

_____

What can you stop doing that isn't giving you a great return on your time and money? (Usually advertising and direct marketing are the first places to look for wasted resources.)

_____

_____

_____

What one or two things can you add to your efforts that would build more/better relationships? Be specific and reasonable. Don't shoot for the moon. Shoot for something you will do regularly and on an ongoing basis.

_____

_____

A Blinding Flash of the Obvious (BFO) is something you might already have known but were reminded of how well it worked for you in the past. What is your BFO from this chapter, and how can you revive the use of that forgotten helpful activity going forward?

_____

_____

Who will you share your Next One Thing with?

_____

_____

_____

When?

_____

_____

Chapter 2

NOBODY WANTS TO BE SOLD, EVERYBODY WANTS TO BUY

For five years, I had made north of $150,000 a year as an Independent Agent. In the year after I implemented the Lumberjack Buying System, my income nearly doubled to $290,000.

—SARAH GOLSON

Meet people where they are, not where you want them to be.

—CHUCK BLAKEMAN

Does anybody ever want to be sold anything? I know I don't. I actively dislike being followed around by the clipboard vultures in a store or having people in a booth at a conference try to convince me I need to stop and meet their need to be listened to.

Nobody wants to be sold anything, yet *everybody* wants to buy. This realization has been haunting the sales process since the Factory System invented the modern pushy salesperson, and multiple sales gurus have rightly written very popular books about it, although they've offered little by way of a relational solution to it. What if we could move away from clever proposals, fancy slide decks, leading questions, or persistent stalking? What if we could actually turn all this around and have them lean into us, wanting to buy? It's more than possible, and it's not even hard. And once you've learned how, you'll never go back to selling "at" people.

The allegory I use for this kind of relational business development is the Lumberjack Buying System, an invitational and attractional way of acquiring Clients who want to buy without being sold.

For the rest of this book, we're going to focus on being invitational and attractional, seeing people not as targets or as contacts that need to be sold, but as people who, when approached relationally with an approach tested by thousands over the past 19 years, will turn the tables and start wanting to buy. To that end, the Lumberjack Buying System is not a selling system. Instead, it helps us meet people where they are and decide when to make them aware what part we can play in meeting their needs. It is designed to help us know exactly where someone is in the three stages of business development and what we can do to help them move to the next stage.

Over the years, I have leaned into this simple secret to acquiring new Clients (and to being a helpful human being):

Meet people where they are, not where you want them to be.

Most sales processes are designed to get people to join you where *you* are. "If they could just understand where I'm coming from, and see how much good I could do for them, I know I could sell to them." It runs counter to logic (and yet it's very intuitive), but we need to learn how to do the opposite. We need to first find out where they are by using very specific questions, learn where they want to end up, and then join them in that process. When you remember to meet people where *they* are and commit to getting them to where *they* want to be, you'll find that they begin to want to buy from you so you won't have to sell "at" them.

The Lumberjack Buying System lays the foundation for this *"Sell Less, Earn More"* approach. Later we'll add things like the Four Walking-In Commitments, the Four Buying Questions, Tier Three Listening, and a couple of other tools that might be business changers (and possibly even life changers) for you. But we can't get to everything at once, so as Rodgers and Hammerstein's "Do-Re-Mi" song goes, "Let's start at the very beginning. It's a very good place to start."

How Sales Begins

There are a lot of important similarities between the classic small business sales cycle in Figure 2.1 below and what we call the Lumberjack Buying System, and we'll be able to more clearly see the vast differences by viewing both. Loosely, this is the classic sales cycle:

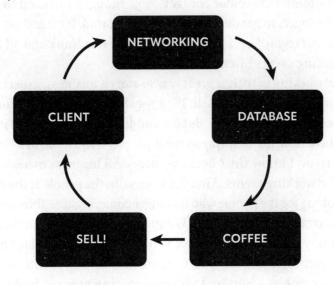

Figure 2.1: The Classic Sales Cycle

The classic sales cycle might start with going to a networking event to search for Customers. Hopefully there are a few people there who might want what you're offering, but you have to work proactively and quickly to sift through many dozens of people to find a few potential Clients. In two hours, you can really only meet a few people unless you're a bit insensitive and very transactional about how you approach them. But let's say it works. You find a possible Client who thinks they might need what you have, you get their contact information, and you both agree to meet for coffee or at an office. You talk, maybe multiple times, and then you present the offer. They buy, and you go back to the networking events for another go-round. It works, but unfortunately, you've just jumped on the sales treadmill and will have trouble ever getting off.

NETWORKING: A PLACE TO BEGIN, NOT A LIFESTYLE

Let me be clear: There's nothing wrong with networking, *at first*. I did it when I first started a business in a city where I didn't think I had potential customer contacts, so I thought I needed to meet more strangers to get the business off the ground. It turned out I was wrong, but regardless, I jumped on the sales treadmill, and off to the networking events I went.

Networking is truly a great way to start a business, especially if you aim to serve and not sell. It's a way to start finding customers, maybe even for a few years. But it shouldn't be a lifestyle, and it's not anywhere near the best way to meet people. It's just the first way.

How do I know this? Because successful business owners don't go to networking events. Almost universally, the people at the events are looking for the people who no longer come, because those owners have learned that networking is a great place to start, but there are better ways to meet people once you have a few good relationships under your belt. Crassly put, in some networking events (not all), I felt like one of a hundred vultures circling around, looking for the dead cow. But that dead cow—that ideal Client with the higher revenue business—no longer showed up because they had found a better way to build their business.

There's a lot of uncomfortable, nonrelational, and highly transactional things that can happen in networking: stabbing each other with business cards, exhibiting superficial personal interest, or scanning the crowd to find that ideal Client and then abruptly abandoning their conversation to go hunt them. And then there is the worst transactional strategy: being stalked because you *are* the ideal Client. It's why some people avoid networking events upfront, even when they could actually be helpful. Nobody wants to be stalked.

However, if you're moving to a new city or leaving a job that involved a lot of travel to start your own business locally, networking is a great way to start. But then let's get you off the sales treadmill. We want you to be one of those business owners whom everyone would love to see at a networking event, but who no longer shows up. You need to outgrow networking and grow into something much more sustainable and rewarding: relationships. As we often put it, very early we should learn how to:

Stop networking and build a network instead.

Successful business owners can stop going to networking events because they have built a very small network of three to five other business owners who have all the Clients they want, and they all share them abundantly with one another.

In contrast, the classic sales cycle feels like a treadmill. I repeated the same five, time-consuming activities in the sales cycle to find one customer at a time. It is not efficient and will eventually wear you down. What if instead we could have a Steady Stream of Potential Clients and outgrow networking forever? This is where I get motivated. I'm ambitiously lazy. I will work my ass off *now* so I don't have to work as hard *later*. You might find that motivating, too.

Instead of endlessly working, let's set the goal of working smarter now, so we can work less later. Let's get off the sales treadmill permanently.

The Lumberjack Buying System

As we explain it, you'll see that the Lumberjack Buying System (LBS) has some similarities to the classic sales cycle. We still go through the process of meeting people, talking to them, and inviting them to be a Client. And then go back to networking to find another. But instead of repeating the cycle, we want to break it. Our aim is to get to where we rarely if ever have to go to networking events because we don't need to meet strangers anymore. We want to create a Steady Stream of Potential Clients by building our own small network. That breaks the cycle of dependency on networking and frees us to grow exponentially with much less effort. It's what successful small business owners and Independent Agents do: They graduate from networking and jump off the treadmill.

Figure 2.2: The Lumberjack Buying System

THE FOREST AND THE OUTSIDE WOODPILE

In our LBS allegory that we've been using for two decades, the Forest is synonymous with networking (see Figure 2.2 above). We initially go to the Forest (the networking event) to find new people to put in our database (trees for our outside woodpile). If we're doing this right, we're not looking for just any tree. (The "fog-a-mirror" test [are they breathing?] is not a good litmus test. More on that later.) If you have a very clear understanding of who your ideal Client is, you go to the Forest looking specifically for, say, cherry or almond trees, and it's very obvious to you when you find them. This is the first way you can make networking more efficient and graduate from it sooner: know precisely whom you are looking for. We'll show you how to get clarity later on.

If we're successful, we get the right person's contact information and carry that home. In our allegory, we've just moved them from the Forest (the networking event) to our own Outside Woodpile (our database). Too often, however, we stall out right here. I have a friend who for years taught a course titled, "A Rubber-Banded Stack of Business Cards Is Not a Marketing Strategy." Enough said. We need to keep the process moving.

TIME KILLS DEALS

Two things are true about this old sales saw. It is absolutely true that time kills deals, which should highly motivate you to keep people moving through the process. But it is equally true that if you don't relax and invest time in seasoning the relationship, asking Jenna to marry you too soon will get a "No." "Time kills deals" and "build relationships" live in a healthy tension that keeps us moving at an appropriate pace.

We lived in New England for nine years, and the first year I was there I bought a wood/coal boiler, chopped some trees down on our land, and stacked them to burn. My neighbor came over while I was in the process and kindly informed me that chopping these trees down in August was not a good strategy for burning them in October. They had not been "seasoned," or dried, and would not burn. Instead, they would just spit, sputter, smoke, and protest loudly when I put them on the fire, much like people do when we're too aggressive with them. I called a guy and bought four cords of seasoned wood. Lesson learned.

This is the first mistake we make in sales. We see everyone with dollar signs on their foreheads and think our job is to separate them from as much of that money as possible, as quickly as possible. Again, it's what we've been taught. But business has never really been transactional (thanks again, Factory System, for this unhelpful detour). With rare exceptions (and no, you aren't one of them), we need to season relationships before we can make requests of them. I'm very comfortable asking people I know for help, and rightly so; but not so much from people I don't. Wood needs to season on the outside woodpile for a while, and relationships need time to develop, too.

That doesn't mean you don't do anything with your digitally rubber-banded stack of business connections. Unlike the wood, you don't season relationships by just letting them sit idle. In Chapter 13, we'll talk about a simple Drip System to season relationships and build trust that takes very little time and energy but offers big returns.

THE INSIDE WOODPILE

Trust is the cornerstone of a seasoned relationship, and we'll show you how to gain trust very early in the Outside Woodpile process. Once you have a seasoned relationship, it is much easier to have a conversation about your product or service and gauge their interest. You might have a few dozen interactions with them while they're on the Outside Woodpile before you finally get to the good stuff. Then they are ready to sit down with you to talk specifically about whether your product or service is a fit for them. We call this a Buying

Conversation, and if you're having one, your potential Client is now on the Inside Woodpile. You're in the house, things are heating up, and you're much closer to them becoming your customer.

ON THE FIRE—YES OR NO

The LBS allegory again serves to remind us that time kills deals. That first winter in New England, I found out you really didn't want wood lying around inside for a couple of weeks because the bugs thought it was spring and started hatching. When a potential Customer or Client is at the point of wanting to discuss your product or service, it's not a good time to let that drop. You need to keep things moving. The closer you get to a decision, generally, the faster things should move, like water moving through a narrowed opening. The fancy term for this in physics is the Venturi effect. The closer you get to the sale, the faster the process should move.

Many times, people move from the Inside Woodpile (Buying Conversation) to On the Fire (OTF) in the same conversation, depending on the average length of your sales cycle, which can range from hours to many months. You will know someone is On the Fire because you have asked them, "Would you like to give it a try?" They are now at the *Yes/No* stage. There's nothing left but to make a decision. If they say, "Well, I need to talk to my partner," that's also valid. But in that case, they jump off the fire and back on to the Inside Woodpile, and you just need to ask them when you can circle back with them. You may go back and forth a few times—On the Fire to Inside Woodpile and back again, knocking down straw men and real obstacles. And when they say yes, that's wonderful: You've got a new Client. Congratulations.

A New Client—A Fork in the Sales Process Road

Here's where we radically diverge from the classic sales funnel. Just because it worked to go find a stranger doesn't mean you should go do it again. At some point, and ideally in well less than a year of networking, you can begin going a very different and energizing direction to find new Clients: back to people you already know. It's likely that most of you have enough existing relationships to either skip networking already or use it as an opening strategy you can drop soon. More on this later.

But wait. There's more . . .

What if you had a reliable process that could allow you to skip the Forest and stop hunting strangers altogether? And over the course of a year or so, what if the process allowed you to even skip your own Outside Woodpile (database, remember) and have potential Customers or Clients show up without having been pursued in any way? This is where it gets fun. The most expensive part of sales in both time and money is on the front end. What if we could greatly reduce or even eliminate that front-end work (see Figure 2.3 below) and the tons of marketing, time, and money it requires?

Figure 2.3: Sales Without Networking—What Successful Business Owners Do

Let's find our Clients somewhere else going forward: from people we already know. When you have three to five Lumberjacks regularly referring people to you and you're no longer going to the Forest to hunt for new Clients, sales is a lot more fun and a lot more effective in growing our business quickly.

Lumberjacks, Not Just Customers

The classic sales process has taught us to always chase the next Client by finding the next stranger. But the easiest and most rewarding way to find your next Client is to connect with someone you already know who has all the Clients you want, isn't in competition with you, and can send you a few Clients at a time for years to come. We call these people Lumberjacks. They've been to the networking Forest and beyond, and over the years they have built a great Outside Woodpile full of potential Clients for you.

At any given time, we all might have 3, 10, or even 20 potential Customers on our list. What if you had 1,400? Your Lumberjacks have great relationships with their existing and past Customers and with other people who are friends and/or Lumberjacks for them. These friends of theirs could all function as the same resource for you. Let's do the math. If you have four Lumberjacks who each have 350 connections on their list, you now have a potential contact list of 1,400, plus the 10 strangers you found by hunting at networking events or by cold calling, plus your own list of contacts. And as you develop the trust of these Lumberjacks, they will be gate openers to the world for you. We'll show you how as we flesh out the Lumberjack Buying System.

Your Competition Is Your Friend

Here's another dirty little secret of relational sales. Some of the people you think are your competitors are going to be the best referral sources, or Lumberjacks, you will ever have. For years we had five accountants from a number of different 3to5 Clubs who got together monthly to pass Clients around. They had learned the 80/20 rule in a new way. We all have niches we prefer, and if I could fill my business with only those specific kinds of Customers, that would be nirvana. These guys found nirvana by sending Customers they thought of as marginal to other accountants, for whom they were ideal. And they were off the sales treadmill.

Another part of the same secret: Your very best Lumberjacks will likely never buy a thing from you. Instead, they will have similar businesses to yours, or professionally at least very "near" yours. Mortgage brokers and realtors make good Lumberjacks, as do CPAs and wealth managers, or a bridal salon and a wedding planner. Or any two renovation companies that specialize in different niches.

This strategy requires a powerful mindset of abundance:

You either live in a world of abundance or in a world of scarcity, and whichever one you choose affects every decision you make.

Choose abundance. We didn't invent this. Zig Ziglar said, "You can have everything in life you want, if you will just help enough other people get what they want." If you commit to serving other business owners and Independent Agents and sending them the Clients they want, it will come back to you. Sadly, a lot of people don't live in a world of abundance, so you will have to sift through these to find your three to five Lumberjacks. But it's worth it, because that's all you need to get off the sales treadmill.

The Few, the Mighty

Having built 13 businesses in 10 different industries and professions using these principles, I am convinced that any business owner can build a great business with just three to five Lumberjacks, their existing and past Clients, and other people they already know who will never buy a thing from them. It may take six months to a year or more if you're just starting out (it might also happen right away), but building Lumberjack relationships will always be more fruitful than going to the Forest and hauling out one tree at a time. Or, to use a classic analogy, we're taught to chase eggs, when what we need to do is make friends with the golden goose. No more egg-chasing, and, in our metaphor, no more going to the Forest to labor over one unseasoned tree.

I'm also convinced there is a Paul Bunyan out there for every business. You may already know yours, you just haven't realized it yet. At one luncheon, a guy told me about a woman business owner who had spent $600,000 on machinery just to start her fledgling business. She connected with him a month later. With her startup expenses and infrastructure costs, she needed $50,000 a month in sales just to break even. He was able to refer $75,000 a month in business to her that would have taken her a year or more to drum up on her own. She found her Paul Bunyan right out of the gate.

To illustrate the power of finding your Paul Bunyan in a different context, there's two ways to sell a book. One is to get in your car and drive around the country doing readings at countless bookstores, sign copies, and sell 5 to 20 books at each store. In doing so, you trust these people will each refer a friend or two. It's a concert tour for authors. The other way is to get Oprah Winfrey, or any other Paul

Bunyan, to simply mention your book. Or be fortunate enough, as I was, to get invited to do a TEDx talk and get a big endorsement. Lumberjacks make life so much easier, so much faster.

Advocates and Raving Fans

As you dive into this system, you'll be able to easily identify two "levels" of Lumberjacks, L1s and L2s (see Figure 2.4 below).

L1s are what I call "Advocates"—they love you and want you to be successful, but you are not at the center of their lives. You need to remind them that you can use their help. And when you do, they love to pitch in. You don't get their help by stalking them but by using the Drip System we mentioned earlier. That makes them want to lean in and connect with you whenever they hear from you. When you connect with them, an Advocate will say something like, "Hey, I just remembered. I met a woman a couple of weeks ago who would be a great [Client or Lumberjack] for you. I'll send an email connecting you both." Advocates are precious, so treat them as such. Remember they're busy, and don't stalk them. Tread lightly in their lives, with welcome acts of Recency and Frequency brought to them one gentle drip at a time.

L2s are the Holy Grail of Lumberjacks. You'll know you're dealing with an L2 because they refer people to you without you asking. You just wake up in the morning and the email is sitting in your inbox: "Roberta, meet Chuck. I highly recommend you get a cup of coffee with him. He could really help your business. Chuck, meet Roberta. I think you might benefit from getting to know her, too."

The Forest	All the people you meet in life (and at networking)
Outside Woodpile	Ideal prospects who gave you contact information Outside Woodpile = Your Database
Inside Woodpile	Buying Conversation
On the Fire	Buying Question: Would you like to give it a try?
Client/Not Client	Ask for referral, be a Lumberjack for them
Lumberjack 1	Advocate: Loves you, but you have to ask for referrals
Lumberjack 2	Raving Fan: Sends you Clients without asking

Figure 2.4: The LBS Process

Connected or Connector?

As a very important aside, in most cases, sadly, your mother is neither a Raving Fan nor an Advocate. A realtor friend once told me her dad was helping her with her taxes when she overheard her mother and her card-playing friends talking about one of them wanting to move. Mom never brought up her daughter, the realtor. She had to get with Mom afterward and force the connection.

As I mentioned before, our Advocates and Raving Fans are almost always people who are close to or in our profession/industry, who can use the 80/20 rule to send us Clients. Mom loves us, but many times she doesn't even understand what we do. Just because people love you doesn't make them a Lumberjack. Mom might be well-connected, but not good at connecting you to those connections. A lot of the more popular, well-known business owners in your area are not good connectors. Don't waste your time with these power players. To find a great Lumberjack, always look for a connectOR, not people who are connectED.

Get Off the Networking Treadmill

Anyone who has ever gotten off the networking treadmill has found Lumberjacks, either deliberately or by trial and error. (When you do it intentionally, it works better.) Business in many countries is more relationship-based than American business, which leans heavily toward being transactional. Let's fix that. The Lumberjack Buying System has been proving itself in the world for a very long time under many names, in many countries.

You might have to connect with quite a few Customers or people in or near your industry before one finally sees the value of building a Lumberjack/keiretsu relationship with you. But as we mentioned before, you only need three to five of them. No more strangers.

I Need Clients Now—Dual-Tracking

If you're just starting up or have hit a slump and need revenue fast, you will likely need to develop Clients as well as Lumberjacks. We call this Dual-Tracking, and you can use the same activities to do both. When I first started Crankset Group in 2006, I went to networking events to find both Customers and Lumberjacks. I intended to develop every customer I found into a Lumberjack if it fit. Be intentional and do both at the same time. Don't just go for customers. You'll get where you want to be a lot faster if you Dual-Track your efforts.

Everything we talk about going forward will help you Dual-Track. You can use these tools and principles to find both Clients and Lumberjacks. It's all about intention. If you intend to find one Client at a time, you will. If you intend to find Oprah Winfrey or your Paul Bunyan, you are much more likely to do so. Once I realized this, my intention became focused on finding great Lumberjacks so I would never have to go to the Forest again. And it worked. I got off the roller-coaster sales treadmill, moved on from networking, and built my businesses with people I already knew.

In one of our 10-week FasTrak business development courses,[5] a realtor told the Facilitator who was running the course that she spent 20 hours or more per week attending networking events and that it had worked quite well for her for a very long time. The FasTrak Facilitator suggested she stop networking for the length of the course and instead simply meet with people she already knew. She didn't like the idea but committed to trying it. After FasTrak was over, she told the Facilitator that her potential Client list had gone up exponentially and she was making a lot more take-home income than before. Interestingly, she also said, "I'm not having as much fun, but I'm definitely enjoying life a lot more." Networking had been just plain fun for her, but building Lumberjack relationships was making the rest of her life much more rewarding.

She had learned a valuable lesson—we need to work to cut out as much of the front of the sales funnel as possible. Finding potential customers is the most time- and capital-intensive part of sales. If you can reduce or eliminate going to the Forest, that's a huge savings of both. And if you can get to where your own database is only a small part of your contacts and other business owners will share theirs with you, you'll be moving with an efficiency and effectiveness that most owners and salespeople only dream of.

Cutting Out the Front End of the Sales Funnel

For many years I held what we called the Business Leader's Insight Lunch, where we took over a large private room, people bought their own lunches, and I shared a business principle to discuss as they ate. All these people very quickly learned the principles in this

---

5   To learn more about FasTrak, visit https://www.3to5club.com/double-your-income/.

book. About six months after starting the BLI Lunch, I arrived at the restaurant to realize I had completely forgotten to send out any emails or texts or make any phone calls to invite people to come that week. And yet more than 35 of them showed up. The next week I intentionally didn't put out any invites, and 40-plus people showed up. People who knew me and found benefit in what we do were inviting and bringing others. My Outside Woodpile had grown from the names I had in my database to all the people they knew as well. Lumberjacks are a great gift to any business.

I have found that the most successful people in business and in life are in some way ambitiously lazy. They don't just endlessly work hard. They work hard upfront so they can figure out how to work less later and get an even better result. I want you to get to the point that not only are you not having to hunt strangers anymore, but your database is also no longer the major source of potential Clients. Let's learn how to gain the trust of those few Lumberjacks we need to build a successful business.

Be ambitiously lazy; work hard *now* to build Lumberjack relationships to get off the sales treadmill for good.

My Next One Thing: The Lumberjack Buying System

How do you know where someone is in the sales cycle? They are:

In the Forest because _____

In the Outside Woodpile because _____

In the Inside Woodpile because _____

On the Fire because _____

Describe your Lumberjack _____

    A Level 1 Lumberjack (L1) is an advocate because _____

    Level 2 Lumberjack (L2) is a Raving Fan because _____

How can you apply Dual-Tracking to your own sales? _____

When someone becomes a Client, what can you do that differs from the traditional sales cycle?

_____

_____

Who will you share your Next One Thing with? _____

_____ When? _____

Chapter 3

RIPE FOR THE PICKING

*Applying the simple principle of Low Hanging Fruit
doubled my monthly income in less than 90 days.*

—Josh McKay

You get what you intend, not what you hope for.

—Chuck Blakeman

How do you begin to build a Lumberjack Buying System to funnel you a Steady Stream of Potential Clients? It starts with the most important marketing strategy you have probably never used: *create a list of everyone you know.* That might sound too simplistic or obvious. It's simple, but it is not simplistic. When I tried it for the first time after 20 years in business, it changed everything. While it doesn't need a lot of explanation, I'm giving it its own short chapter to emphasize its importance.

When I say make a list of everyone you know, I mean *everyone*, including the baby-sitter, the dog-sitter, and the next-door neighbors. There are two reasons to do this. First, we need to break out of our stale mindset around who we think is our Client and then narrow it back down later. Second, and much more important, you need to realize that the baby-sitter's mother and the neighbor's adult son *are* your ideal Client, or a potential Lumberjack, or they know someone who is. Again, we have been taught to chase Clients directly, but a not-so-well-kept secret of business development is the principle of one to two degrees of separation from your ideal Client (not six degrees; it's almost never six).

Start by listing everyone in your head and in your life. Then ask yourself the all-important, one-degree-of-separation question: "Who do they know who might be a Customer or a Lumberjack?" Then stretch it an even more important second degree: "Who do they know *who might know someone* who could be right for me?" It's at the second degree that a lot of magic can happen. Maybe the baby-sitter and their parents aren't the answer, but the baby-sitter's mother knows someone who has all the Clients you could want, wouldn't see you as a competitor, and would be willing to introduce you. If you had continued to dismiss the baby-sitter because you "knew" they couldn't help your business, you would have missed that connection.

One caveat: For those of us inclined to Play Office (yeah, I'm one of them), stop when your list of names gets to 50 or 100. You can continue to build it after you have actually started connecting with people on the list. When I first tried this method, I used the excuse of waiting until I had everyone I knew included before I did anything else. As they say, it's paralysis by analysis.

The Hawthorne Effect and Pearson's Law

The Factory System folks did get some things right. An early 20th-century idea, Pearson's Law, gives us a principle to help you double your income by making a list of everyone you know. The principle is this:

That which is measured, improves. That which is measured and reported back, improves exponentially.

They didn't know this back then, but just writing things down does something positive neurologically. Keeping track of what we write down and updating it is a surefire way to build revenue fast. Another way to look at it is you are gamifying work.

Putting This to Work on the Ground

Sarah Golson sold coupon advertising that showed up in your mailbox in a blue envelope, which is never an easy gig. For five straight years, she had made around $150,000 a year doing it. She went through our FasTrak course with the intention of doubling her income. After 90 days, she was on a $300,000 run rate, exactly the ambitious goal she had intended when she started the course. A year later, she had "only" done $290,000 that year, not quite double. But imagine what that did for her lifestyle, since most of that increase was disposable income.

Sarah's secret? After years of successful sales, she went back and wrote down a list of everyone she knew and began to manage it with our Lumberjack Buying System report. She laughingly said she was doing so well she could have quit FasTrak the first week instead of finishing the 10-week course. She had no idea how much Low Hanging Fruit she had created over the years without pulling it across the finish line. I had a similar experience when I first tried it.

You will always have Low Hanging Fruit—people you just got too busy or too distracted to move all the way to On the Fire (at the Yes/No stage). Low Hanging Fruit never goes away, though, and reviewing your Low Hanging Fruit list will be an invaluable reminder through the years of people you have not yet fully served.

Be intentional. Make a list of *everyone* you know. It is the simple foundation of building your business quickly and it might even result in you doubling your income or revenue in 90 days.

You get what you intend, not what you hope for.

I'll be talking a lot about being intentional throughout the rest of this book. Start first with intending to uncover everyone you already know.

My Next One Thing: Low Hanging Fruit

Which present client/customer presents the best opportunity for you to grow your business with them?

_____

What is the Next One Thing you will do to increase your revenue with that present customer? _____

_____ By when? _____

Which past client/customer presents the best opportunity for you to bring them back? _____

_____

What is the Next One Thing you will do to reconnect with that past client/customer? _____

_____ By when? _____

Is there a proposal that is stalled? If so, what is the Next One Thing you will do to move it forward? _____

_____ By when? _____

Identify one potential Lumberjack who is most likely to be able to refer someone to you quickly. What is the Next One Thing you will do to strengthen that relationship and get that referral?

_____

_____ By when? _____

Figure 3.1 below shows an example of a Low Hanging Fruit report you could use to make a list, or you can get ours at 3to5club.com/SDS.

Your Single Most Valuable Marketing Strategy

LOW HANGING FRUIT – Make a list of all the people you know in each category, and a plan to start connecting with them.

Also consider your prices and/or collecting on receivables.

	Present Customers (Upsell)	Present Prospects Pending	Past Customers (Upsell, resell)	Old/State Proposals	Alliance Partners / Friends	Advocates (like me) / Raving Fans (refer me)	Raise Prices / Reduce Costs	Collect Receiv.! Fire Clients, Change Process
Your Primary Product or Service								
Your Secondary Product or Service								

Figure 3.1: Low Hanging Fruit—Your Single Most Valuable Marketing Strategy

Chapter 4

IT COULDN'T BE THIS SIMPLE, COULD IT?

The key to success is to know exactly what you are doing,
where you are going, and how you will get there.

— Anonymous

The most important number you will ever
know in business: your First Domino.

—Chuck Blakeman

The classic sales funnel (see Figure 4.1 below) goes something like this: You connect with 10 people to see if they'll meet with you, three of them agree, and one of those becomes a Client. I don't know who came up with these numbers, but I'm sure they work for somebody. Maybe even you. My numbers have always been different.

THE CLASSIC **SALES FUNNEL**

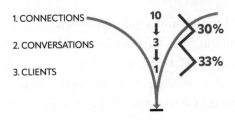

Figure 4.1: The Classic Sales Funnel

We need to stop here and ask whether you know the three numbers that make up *your* sales funnel? We call these the Three C's of business development:

1. **Connections.** How many people do you need to Connect with to get one Buying Conversation?
2. **Conversations.** How many (Buying) Conversations or cups of coffee does it take for you to bring on one new Client/Customer?
3. **Customers/Clients.** How many new Customers/Clients per week/month do you need to grow successfully and get off the treadmill? (The answer to this one informs the two above.)

From my experience, less than one out of 20 business owners or Independent Agents can answer even one of those three vital questions. And yet we're all out there in the networking forest, madly hunting any stranger who can fog a mirror and then stabbing them with our business cards. We're all deeply and unconsciously committed to what I've come to call the Random Hope Strategy of Business: "I'm going to work really hard and hope something good happens." But clarity is power, and without these answers, you have neither clarity nor power. We need to be very intentional about uncovering our Three C's.

Your First Domino

What if we had more than *some* clarity—what if we actually had Utter Clarity about how hard we needed to work to double our income in 90 days? What if the answers to these three questions could help us build a successful, growing business that would give us Freedom IN our business, not FROM it—answers that would help us build a business we love and have a life, too? The answers to the Three C's will reveal:

The most important number you will ever figure out in business—your First Domino.

In every business, there is a First Domino: that single proactive thing you will do that kick-starts everything else in business. We've all seen videos of domino chains: By simply tipping the first domino, it sets in motion a chain reaction that builds on itself, creating its own momentum and making every result in front of it an almost foregone conclusion.

What is your First Domino? What is that one activity you can do that allows you to connect with a potential Customer? When you find it, it will have that domino effect. Because it happened, you can then have a Buying Conversation, which leads to acquiring a new Customer, which results in you being able to (for example) order your chair parts, build the chair, deliver the chair, deposit the payment in your bank account, buy groceries, and go on vacation. All the dominos will fall if we can just identify the first one.

Before I had Utter Clarity on my First Domino, I was just Pigpen from the Charlie Brown cartoons, out there kicking up a lot of dust and making a mess. Random Hope was my first and last name, and during this period of blind groping, I learned the Random Hope Strategy of Business has two specific intentions and one general hope:

1. I intend to work really hard.
2. I intend to make some money.
3. I hope it all works out.

But you get what you intend, not what you hope for. And unfortunately, I got exactly what I had intended: hard work, and *some* money. But for many businesses in a row, I did not get what I hoped for. It never just "worked out." I was always on the treadmill chasing the next sale, feeling like a hostage to my business. It seemed as though I didn't own it, but it owned me.

I had it all backwards. I assumed I could not *intend* for success to "work out" because there are too many variables for me to control. And it's true that we can't fully control outcomes, but that's why I don't say, "You get what you expect." Expectation has a sense of entitlement to it. Intention is not about fully controlling the *outcome* but controlling my *activity* to achieve whatever outcome I am intending. If I don't get the outcome I wanted, can I look at myself and ask, "Did I do everything within my power to make it happen?" That is the power of intention. If I intend to double my income in 90 days, what am I doing to make that happen? I ask this with full awareness that the world might get in the way and make it less or even more than double. But I can be intentional about controlling whatever I can.

Finding My First Domino

When I first used the Three C's process for myself, I followed Stephen Covey's advice to "begin with the end in mind." My "end in mind" was an intention to acquire one new customer every week. That would allow me to break even in 12 months and start making a profit. With that end in mind, I intuitively threw 35/5/1 against the wall as my Three C's, with very little data to support it:

- **Connections:** 35 people a week in my Outside Woodpile via email, text, phone, and in-person meetings. Schedule a cup of coffee and discuss whether we might find a way to push each other forward.

- **Conversations (Buying):** With no data yet, I intuited that if I had five of these Inside Woodpile (Buying) Conversations every week and asked the Buying Question, "Would you like to give it a try?" (On the Fire), I would acquire . . .
- **Customers:** One per week, from my five (Buying) Conversations and OTF questions.

What was my First Domino? When I put the above Three C's into action, I soon found that my First Domino was centered on Buying Conversations. To acquire one new Client per week, I resolved that my intention was to have five Buying Conversations every week. That was my First Domino.

Again, I had no solid basis for deciding this, but as Albert Einstein said, "Intuition is the highest form of human intelligence," and good business owners rely on it regularly, sometimes to interpret data, but especially when you have none. To begin with, try using your intuition to come up with the numbers for your Three C's, like I did above. You might be surprised later how close you were to the correct numbers once you use the faithful servant of rational data to keep track for a while.

There are two closing ratios you see in our Three C's above. If you connect with 10 people with the intention of having a Buying Conversation with three of them, and that happens, you have a 30 percent closing ratio from Connections to Conversations. If you have three Buying Conversations and intend to get one Client, and you do, your closing ratio for Conversations to Clients/Customers is 33 percent. One of those first two activities, either Connections or (Buying) Conversations, will be your First Domino—the most important number/activity you will ever figure out for your business.

You'll notice that I keep putting "Buying" with "Conversation." You'll have plenty of non-buying conversations with people who are still on the Outside Woodpile. The only ones we track as "Conversations" in the second "C" are ones where the conversation is about what we have to offer. All the other earlier "Outside Woodpile" conversations are great Recency and Frequency warm-ups to get you to that point. And as you'll learn in Chapter 6, using the Woodpile Buying System, you can begin to meet people for the first time who already like you because you were highly referred by someone they already like as well.

The Three C's for Lumberjacks

As we've mentioned, what is ideal is for us to find three to five trusting Lumberjacks rather than hunt 300 to 500 individual Clients. You'll get Clients from your Lumberjacks, which include your existing and past Clients and people you know who will never buy a thing from you. So we Dual-Track and use the Three C's to find Customers if we need them quickly, and at the same time, we use those Three C's to discover our Lumberjacks.

A closing Conversation with a Lumberjack might sound like, "I've got Clients you might want; you have Clients I might be able to serve, would you like to see how we can push each other forward?" And a "sale" happens not when they say yes to that but *only* when they refer you to someone who actually becomes a Customer. Until then, they are learning how to refer to you. And if it seems like they're bad at it, they're not. They're trying, and that alone is amazing. You just need to invest a little more time in helping them understand who they should refer to you.

Experiencing Utter Clarity—My First Domino

When I first started Crankset Group in 2006, my loving spouse, Diane, would occasionally ask the most aggravating and seemingly nonsensical question: "How does next month look?" My internal response, "How in the world should I know? It hasn't happened yet!" I would then come up with some tortuous, long-winded Random Hope story of working hard. In sales, we call this a Distraction Strategy.

In 2006, someone said to me, "Success is actually quite predictable." Being an optimist, I loved and embraced this right away. And then, after a little experience applying it, I added a crucial modifier: "... if you're doing the right things." Success and failure are *both* quite predictable, depending on what we're doing.

Seth Godin wrote a book called *The Dip*, in which he described how unsuccessful people did the same unhelpful thing over and over, while others tried that unhelpful thing a couple of times, realized it was insanity, and moved on to find a better way. Random Hope is a predictable cul-de-sac of failure. What if we knew *exactly* what to do to succeed? Then, and only then, is success quite predictable.

The First Domino provides us with that predictability. After a couple of months of tracking my Three C's, I realized the power of my First Domino. I didn't even wait for Diane to ask. "Do you want to know how next month looks?" I eagerly offered. (Her quizzical look said she wasn't thinking about it at all.) I forged ahead. "Well, I need four new Clients per month to grow the way we want to grow. I've been doing this Three C's thing for a few months now, and my ratio of Buying Conversations to new Customers is about four to one, or actually 27.8 percent. I just need four cups of coffee a week with potential Clients. Right now, I have five set up for the first week of next month, three for the second and third weeks, and two for the fourth week. I just need four more appointments, and next month will be great." She was pleased and thankful I had clarity. Utter Clarity.

Some psych people say, "The worst of human conditions is uncertainty." That's why being a hostage for three months is so much worse than being a prisoner for the same amount of time. Not knowing what our future holds can be nerve-racking. (I also strongly believe it's the best of human conditions and the only way we grow, but that's for another time.) What if you knew with relative certainty that next month would be great? Rather than working really hard and hoping something good happens, you could work very deliberately and precisely and believe you would achieve what you're shooting for.

Now imagine what that felt like for me. When I achieved Utter Clarity, it was both exhilarating and scary. It was exhilarating because, taking into account the law of averages week to week, I finally knew *exactly* what I needed to do to grow my business. But it was scary for the same reason—I knew *exactly* what I needed to do to grow my business. Clarity isn't always sunshine and rainbows.

At times in my life, I have been "professionally confused." I would think, "I don't know what to do, there are so many things I could do that might work, and so many that could just lead me down a cul-de-sac . . . I just don't know what to do." And either fear and paralysis would set in, or I would go into Pigpen mode and start employing the Random Hope Strategy of Business all over again.

Knowing that I just needed five cups of coffee a week cleared the fog. I went from "I just don't know what to do" to "Great, I know exactly what to do." But then I thought, "Oh no. I know exactly what to do." "Oh no" was arguing with "Great." Utter Clarity had removed all my "Playing Office" excuses. So I was going to find out very quickly if I really wanted the business I had said I wanted and if "Great" would win out over "Oh no." My desire was now going to be tested by the reality of getting up every morning and saying, "Well, I know exactly what to do today. So, there's only one question left to answer. Am I going to do it, or not? Am I going to get my five cups of coffee, or not?"

Are you?

Are You Analog or Digital?

After finding my First Domino, my world changed from one full of endless possibilities to one where I had to answer one simple yes or no question every morning. I have since adopted the concept that I went from an analog world to a digital one. In the analog world, we use zero through 9 to create an infinite set of numbers and possibilities. In the digital world, there are only two numbers: "one," which equates to yes, and "zero," which equates to no. My world had been reduced to one (am I going to set up five coffees?) and zero (I don't want this bad enough); yes or no. Utter simplicity. Utter Clarity. No more excuses. I was now in a position to find out if I really wanted a successful business or not.

We're still here a couple of decades later, so you know how it turned out. It was simple; it just wasn't easy.

As I developed Lumberjack relationships, I quickly found I didn't need a ratio of 35/5/1, but more like 20/5/1. As I got better at the whole process, within a few more months it was more like 10/5/1 or even lower. My Conversations to Clients was closer to four to one. Around 27.8 percent of the potential Clients I talked to became a Client (out of the first 194 Buying Conversations I had, 54 people bought something, or 27.8 percent). I had a friend who was always well north of 35 percent with his Conversation to Client conversions, and I had to remind myself not to compare my numbers to his. Yours will be different, too. Just focus on improving.

As you can see by my closing ratio of 27.8 percent, I really didn't need five cups of coffee a week—more like four. So why did I keep doing five? Because if I scheduled four cups of coffee, there are a lot of reasons why I might only end up with three: it snowed, someone had a sick child, the dog ate something it shouldn't have, my best Client called with a problem, etc. If that had happened, I could have just said, "Well, it's not *my* fault. I scheduled four cups of coffee."

But because I knew this kind of thing would happen at times, I took responsibility to mitigate against it with five scheduled meetings. I'll say it again, "You get what you intend, not what you hope for," and being intentional means doing everything in your power to allow something great to happen. If somebody cancels on me, I still have four meetings. And if nobody does, that's great! I've got five and I'm one ahead. Don't be a victim of things you can control with just a little foresight.

Gaining Utter Clarity

Do you want to know your First Domino? You won't find it on a spreadsheet. Get out there and start talking to people you already know. Do so with the intention to create Connections and (Buying) Conversations so you can acquire Customers/Clients. Track each of these three activities in any way you find useful: on a napkin, in a fancy database, anything that allows you to add them up. We'll show you how to make these Connections and have those Conversations later with the Four Walking-In Commitments and the Four Buying Questions.

To get started, just intuitively throw something against the wall like I did so you can get moving. I have learned something through the decades:

It is never how good your plan is that matters, but how committed you are to the result you intend.

The question isn't whether you've got a great plan, but whether it's better than the plan you didn't have before and whether you are committed to getting to your goal.

We'll use the rest of this book to show you how to find people to have coffee with. The process will be different for everyone. For now, commit yourself to becoming digital. As soon as you figure out your First Domino, begin to say "Yes" to it every morning and be prepared to get what you want from your business.

My Next One Thing: Your First Domino and Other Critical Numbers

If you have a feel for your two critical closing ratios as they exist now, record them here. If you don't have hard numbers, make an educated, intuitive guess.

CONNECTIONS TO CONVERSATIONS

On average I connect with _____ people per week (in-person, calls, emails, texts, talks, videos, events, etc.), and from that, I am able to schedule _____ (Buying) Conversations. (Reminder: The other person is aware you will be sharing your product or service and asking them to consider working with you.)

CUSTOMERS TO CLIENTS

On average I acquire one new Client or Customer for every _____ Buying Conversations I have. (If it takes two weeks to acquire a Customer, multiply your weekly Buying Conversations by two.)

Therefore, right now, my two most important business development closing ratios are below.

(Divide the second number by the first number. For example, 4 Conversations divided by 12 Connections = 33 percent closing ratio.)

_____ Connections to _____

Conversations is _____%

_____ Conversations to _____

new Clients/Customers is _____%

You can use this formula to focus on end Clients, find Lumberjacks, or both, depending on your current goals. If you're Dual-Tracking and looking for end Clients while you build your Lumberjack network, you can create ratios for both.

What is your Blinding Flash of the Obvious from this chapter, and how will you apply it?

_____

Who will you share your Next One Thing with? _____

_____ When? _____

In the next chapter, we'll use these two simple ratios to help you discover the most important number you will ever know in business—your First Domino.

Chapter 5

THE MOST IMPORTANT
NUMBER YOU'LL EVER KNOW

*Six weeks into applying the principles, practices, and tools in
Sell Less, Earn More, I'm beginning to gain real clarity on what
I actually need to do to grow my business of 20 therapists. The
Random Hope Strategy doesn't apply to me anymore. I don't have
to work crazy hard and hope something good happens. Knowing
my First Domino shows us all exactly what to do to be successful.*

—Adria Briggs, owner and clinical director, Experience Growth

*Most business owners work from the Random Hope
Strategy of Business: I'm going to work really hard, and I
hope something good happens. There is a better way.*

—Chuck Blakeman

Now that we know the importance of a First Domino, let's
find yours.

Because I'm a geek who can easily waste time Playing Office by
creating spreadsheets, I built The Leading Indicator Tracker (see
Figure 5.1 below) to help me find my First Domino quickly. You can
do the same—all you really need is a napkin, a piece of paper, your
own spreadsheet, or a computational AI bot. Or, if you want to follow

along with the spreadsheet I'll be using in this chapter, you can get a copy here: 3to5club.com/SDSE.

Your **THREE Cs**

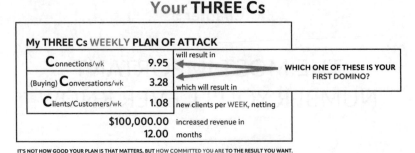

Figure 5.1: The Leading Indicator Tracker

The above is a screenshot of the results at the bottom of my spreadsheet after I plug in just seven numbers. That's all you need—seven numbers. Five of them came from data I already had, and in the beginning, the other two were my two intuitive darts I would throw regarding conversion ratios. But true to the principle that *movement creates the plan*, those intuitive numbers became solid data very quickly as well.

I'll show you how it works. Plug in your five numbers and two assumptions as the first step to gaining Utter Clarity on what your First Domino should be. If you're just starting out (congratulations—fall in love with the journey), either go with all intuitive numbers or find someone who has already been down your road who will share their experience with you.

My advice would be to not use someone else's numbers. Instead, develop your own numbers, processes, and results first, and then check them against other people's experiences. Even if yours are wildly different, that doesn't necessarily mean you've gone down a rabbit hole. It just means you should check your assumptions again. You might just find you're on to something fresh. But if you start by looking at what everyone else has done, you create a box for yourself.

Then don't be surprised if you end up right where they did. *Make your own business rules*, because those who make the rules win.

Let's go through seven steps of the spreadsheet one by one (see Figure 5.2 below):

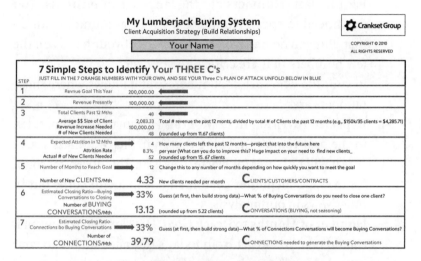

Figure 5.2: My Leading Indicator Tracker

1. **Revenue Goal This Year.** Figure this out first. Where do you want to be in 12 months? Start now instead of waiting until January 1 to decide—that's just Playing Office. It might be a revenue number, a profit number, or an income number. (Income is not profit; profit stays in the business after you take out your income.) What do you intend (not hope or expect) to happen this year? Plug that number in on line 1. For our purposes in this exercise, it's easier to start with revenue and extrapolate profit or income from that. So let's start with revenue.

2. **Revenue Presently.** This is the number you get from adding up your revenue for the past 12 months. Write that number down on line 2.

3. **Total Clients Past 12 Months**. Again, this is easy data to get and plug in here. And if you can't get this or Step 2 above quickly from your own records or your accountant's, it tells you that you are in full-on Random Hope Strategy mode. Fix this fast. Numbers are the language of business. You don't need to speak Numberese—your accountant can do that. But you do need to know how to get your hands on the few numbers that are critical to your success. Get someone in your life who speaks Numberese and knows where those numbers are.

4. **Expected Attrition in 12 Months**. How many customers left in the past 12 months? Plug that in in Step 4, unless you're sure it will be better (or worse) this year. This doesn't account for average spend per customer, but that will come out in other ways in our analysis.

5. **Number of Months to Reach Goal**. How long do you intuit it should take you to get from today's revenue number to your intended goal? And how should you arrive at this number? My rule of thumb is that objectives like these should be "seeable, doable, and slightly scary." If you can't see some kind of path to get to your desired revenue number in, say, six months, then it's just an optimistic guess. Be intuitive instead. Remember, intuition is your highest form of human intelligence.

Even if it's still a bit fuzzy but you can "sort of" see how you might make it happen in 12 months, that's a good start. Then test it—is it slightly scary, very scary, or not at all scary? More often than not, I will go with something slightly scary that I can at least vaguely see happening. Anything less will not give you the urgency you need, and anything more might paralyze you. If your vision becomes clearer as you move, you can always adjust the goal.

6. **Expected Closing Ratio—for This Ration, Buying Conversations to Customers** we're in full on intuition mode

in Step 6. But you're not just fine intuiting a number here—as we discussed in Chapter 4, it's really the best way to get started. It's not taking a shot in the dark, throwing a dart blindfolded, or pulling a number out of your ass. Really go deep inside yourself and find the closing percentage you believe is your best shot, even with no present data. And then check back later to see how close you were. You might be surprised at the accuracy of your intuition.

7. **Expected Closing Ratio—Connections to Buying Conversations**. I plugged this percentage in after I intuited my Conversations to Customers ratio in Step 6 because I use that ratio to help me back into this one. If I believe one out of four people I meet with will buy something from me, then the number above would be 25 percent. And now in Step 7, I feel comfortable asking myself, "How many people do I believe (or intuit) I will need to connect with each week to get four cups of coffee/Conversations?" Figure out your Conversations to Customers ratio first and then intuit this percentage.

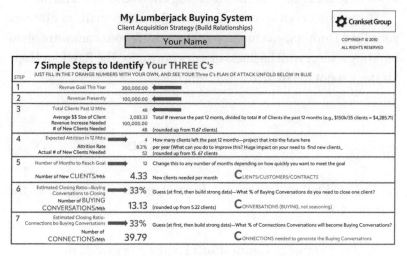

Figure 5.3: My Leading Indicator Tracker

So in the example in Figure 5.3 above, if we desire $200,000 in revenue and are currently at $100,000 with 48 existing Clients, minus an anticipated attrition rate of four Clients per year, then we need 52 new Clients this year to get to $200,000. That breaks down to 4.33 new Clients per month, or roughly one per week. If we believe we can get 33 percent of the people we Connect with into a Conversation, and we believe 33 percent of those will become new Clients, then we need 40 Connections per month, or about 10 per week, and we will acquire one new Client per week.

Let me end this process with this: I flunked ninth-grade algebra, didn't even attempt higher-level math courses, went to music school, and was ADHD and dyslexic. I don't like numbers per se. But I *love* that numbers help me live a freer and more significant life. And it's a huge relief to know there are only a very few numbers any of us really need to know to run a business. Richard Branson, by his own admission, couldn't read a P&L or balance sheet until he already owned many companies and was highly successful. But from the beginning he was a master at figuring out which numbers he needed to know to hit a goal and then focusing all his energy on them.

If you don't even want to do the rudimentary math to discover your First Domino, you might want to rethink your commitment to building a successful business or sales portfolio. The Random Hope Strategy is not the path to a fulfilling life.

Your First Domino

As I've said before, everyone's First Domino will be one of the first two C's:

1. the number of **Connections** I make every week; or
2. the number of **(Buying) Conversations** I need to have this week.

One of these two numbers will motivate you more than the other. I find that most people like pegging weekly "Connections" as their First Domino, which makes sense, because it truly is the first activity you must do to see everything else fall in place for a sale. For almost a year, that was my First Domino as well, but gradually I found I was actually more motivated by using (Buying) Conversations as my First Domino.

I wasn't as motivated by connecting as I was by actually meeting to talk with someone. The scary part was that I now had to commit to keep relentlessly connecting until I got my five cups of coffee per week. As it turned out, because I didn't really enjoy connecting as much as the conversations that followed, I got really good at it, so I could get it done fast and move on to the fun part. It's all a game, and you'll figure out your best approach by simply getting moving.

Is This a Bad Plan?

Your first thought might be, "This is a pretty bad plan. There are some big assumptions here." You are correct. So the real question becomes, "Is this better than the plan I didn't have 15 minutes ago?" If so, then get going, because we already know planning doesn't create movement—movement creates the plan. You'll receive Utter Clarity from movement, not from filling in this spreadsheet. A Bad Plan executed is still better than a great one you never do anything about. We'll talk more about the benefits of Bad Plans later.

In this chapter, you created some very powerful intuitive magic by plugging in just seven numbers. In the coming weeks, as you redirect your Random Hope Strategy energy to this focused work, you will gain Utter Clarity on your First Domino. It might be different from your friend's, but it will always be either your number of Connections or your number of weekly Conversations.

Once you know your First Domino, it becomes just a digital game of Yes every morning. Congratulations. For the first time, your success is quite predictable, because you know you're doing the right thing. And in Chapter 6, we'll show you how to build more confidence that you're doing the right thing.

My Next One Thing: Your First Domino

From this chapter's Leading Indicator Tracker exercise, what is your First Domino? It will either be a specific number and type of Connections or a specific weekly number of (Buying) Conversations.

_____

What is your Blinding Flash of the Obvious from this chapter, and how will you apply it to your business?

_____

Who will you share your Next One Thing with? _____

_____ When? _____

Chapter 6

COMPLICATION KILLS DEALS

As soon as I dumped my complicated CRM system and started
using the Lumberjack Buying System, the amount of activity
I put into sales went down and revenue started going up.

—Sandy Delaney, Pilates for You, LCC

We are addicted to complication and will pay twice as much
for it, when right in front of us is the power and elegance of
simplicity that we ignore because it just can't be that simple.

—Chuck Blakeman

A three-module course with one hour of video instruction can't
possibly be worth more than a course with 10 modules and
six hours of video. A simple one-page spreadsheet can't possibly be
more effective than a full-blown customer relationship management
(CRM) database. Or could it? Do you really need to know someone's
dog's birthday to get them across the finish line?

Keep the Dog Out of Business Development

One Client, who along the way became a friend, made a living selling
the leading CRM. After years of success, he circled back and found

that less than 10 percent of the companies and salespeople who had bought this very expensive software were using it. They said it was too complicated to figure out. He saw a business opportunity, quit his job, and set up shop training salespeople for giant corporations to use CRM. He was very successful, and companies loved his service.

After a few years, he circled back again and found that all his efforts had barely moved the needle. Still, almost no one was using the software. So he quit his training business and instead set up a company that provided the first two of the Three C's. He made all the Connections and set up the Conversations. Then the salespeople just showed up and did their dog and pony shows. (That's actually the best use of a giant corporation salesperson—closing, not hunting.)

But today CRMs are more popular than ever. You'd think they actually worked, and in specific, narrow situations, they do. One of my companies had a 12- to 18-month sales cycle, and once a company came onboard, they could be our Clients for years if not decades, with dozens of people in their company working with us. Managing this complex sales cycle and multiple relationships at one company could be dizzying, and a CRM was a very valuable resource in this context.

But they're called *Customer* Relationship Management systems for a reason. Their main purpose is not helping you sell but helping you retain existing Clients. More often than not, I think sales support is something the CRMs keep trying to tack on to make them seem more valuable.

The greatest strength of CRMs, their ability to capture everything, is also their greatest weakness when it's used to move sales forward. Sales managers in giant corporations love this, because it is easier to report endless activity up the food chain and use that to justify their existence. But small business owners and Independent Agents don't need to know when a potential Client's dog's birthday is to get them across the finish line. We really just need to know five things:

1. Who they are
2. How to contact them
3. What they desire (or what they actually need)
4. The next step we will take to move them forward in the sales cycle
5. When we'll do Step 4

In most sales cycles, anything beyond these five steps is almost always a distraction, not a help. The exception is very long, high-revenue B2B sales cycles—and those make up a very small percentage of the sales world. So, as with just about everything in life, the very complicated CRMs everybody says will save the world won't even save sales. We small business people need something exponentially simpler and focused solely on sales, not on customer relationships. (We will address customer relationships for small businesses in Chapter 13 when we talk about Drip Systems, which focus on regularly serving customers, like CRMs, but without the Fort Knox of data.)

Apparently most salespeople agree. Research shows that more than half of salespeople don't use the company's CRM. From my experience, it's almost always the *best* salespeople—who aren't using the CRM. Great salespeople are mold-breakers, who simplify and focus like a laser on what is actually important.[6]

Again and again, research has found that the best salespeople focus on four things, and most of all on the fourth one:

1. Finding qualified prospects
2. Determining potential needs
3. Offering solutions
4. Closing sales

---

6 Adoption of CRM has increased significantly over the years as managers made it mandatory so *they* could show their effectiveness up the food chain. Remove the manager stick, though, and there is no carrot for using most CRMs to aid the sales process.

One thing gets in the way of these critical functions more than anything else—administrative data input. You're too busy capturing data that obscures what you really need to be doing to close the sale.

In 2022, Salesforce Inc.—yes, the company that makes one of those way-too-complex CRMs you probably shouldn't use—released their annual "State of Sales" report. They found that most CRM-driven people invest only 28 percent of their time in the above four activities. They spend (not invest) the rest of their time Playing Office—recording dogs' birthdays and other data that will be really helpful for long-term B2B customer relationships, but has no relevance to the sales process. Hubspot reports that salespeople who actually do use their CRMs, spend about 96 minutes every day typing in a box to populate them, and spend only one-third of their time selling. Is it any wonder we're not growing our businesses?

We had a CRM to record dogs' birthdays for our B2B fulfillment business. Yet even then, we still kept a simple spreadsheet of people to move multimillion-dollar, long-cycle sales forward. We brought on many giant international companies with that simple spreadsheet. Over the years I've expanded the old axiom "Less is more" to:

When we capture everything, we do nothing.

For small business owners and Independent Agents, it's helpful to capture only what is necessary to move someone through each of the four stages of the Lumberjack Buying System, from Forest to Outside Woodpile to Inside Woodpile to On the Fire and finally to Client. After they become long-term Clients with multiple contacts at their office, then you can plug them into your fancy CRM. Until then, keep it simple.

So what do we really need to capture to move someone through the Lumberjack Buying System? The answer is very, very little.

The Few, the Mighty, the Simple

Please note, I'm not anti-systems. I'm a big proponent of data-driven and process-driven systems tools. I reject the Random Hope Strategy of Business in favor of solid data, using a Leading Indicator Tracker, finding your First Domino, keeping a simple two-page Strategic Plan for your business that you update weekly, and simple written processes for operations we call Freedom Mapping. At the same time, I also understand that complicated systems are rarely the answer. Occam's razor generally applies here: When faced with two possible solutions, the simpler one is usually right.

As mentioned above, with very few exceptions (and you aren't one of them), most of us need just a few bits of data to bring most Customers across the finish line in the business development process. The rest is noise, distraction, and Playing Office.

So What Do We Need?

To build a great business development pipeline, we need about seven things, depending on your specific business. Below in Figure 6.1 is an example of the spreadsheet I used for the first few years I did sales for my own companies; I've been sharing this with business owners and independent salespeople for a couple of decades now in our FasTrak business development program. This is the spreadsheet that reminds us of the Next One Thing we need to do to move someone from the Outside Woodpile to the Inside Woodpile to On the Fire to becoming a Client. The Leading Indicator Tracker helps you define your First Domino, which is a very different bit of data.

To download this spreadsheet and follow along as I illustrate it, go to 3to5club.com/SDSE.

Lumberjack Buying System Tracking

PLANNING DOESN'T CREATE MOVEMENT, MOVEMENT CREATES THE PLAN — GET MOVING AND PLAN AS YOU GO!

Track Your Pipeline (Relationship-Building) Activity Here

Note — the Outside Woodpile category should be large enough that you must keep it on a separate spreadsheet or database. In that case, put only the most likely next prospects here.

Name	Lumberjack (Adv/RF) or Direct Prospect (DR)	Company	Phone #	Email	Simple Action needed to move them to Next Stage.	WHAT IS THE RED FLAG? (the one thing that could stop progress — deal with it!)	Next Contact Date	Possible Revenue Per Year	Date Moved to Next Stage

Outside Woodpile — likely prospects that you have not started a buying conversation with yet. THIS IS THE MOST IMPORTANT CATEGORY TO KEEP FILLED!! IF IT'S EMPTY, ALL OTHER CATEGORIES DRY UP.

								Possible Revenue	Date Moved
1								$-	8-15-20
2								$-	8-15-20
							SUBTOTAL	$-	

Inside Woodpile — In conversation with them about doing work — get them a quote as soon as possible (move to Logs on Fire when quoted)

								Possible Revenue	Date Moved
1								$-	8-15-20
2								$-	8-15-20

Figure 6.1: Lumberjack Buying System Report

Name, Company, Phone Email. We need just the basic contact information—name, company name, and whatever you need to connect with them, such as phone, email, mailing address, URL, or similar. Until we have this, potential Clients are just in the Forest. When we get this information, we can move them to the Outside Woodpile. Then the "time kills deals" clock starts ticking for making the Connection to schedule a (Buying) Conversation.

Lumberjack (ADV/RF) or Direct Prospect (DR). What is my intention for them? For example: 1) To be a Direct Prospect (Customer or Client), 2) To be a Lumberjack (Adv for Advocate, RF for Raving Fan), or 3) Both. Remember, you're more likely to get what you intend than what you hope for. (Yeah, people hear that from me in person a lot, too.)

Single Action Needed to Move Them to Next Stage. What is the Next One Thing (not three things) I will do to move them from whatever stage they are in to the next stage in the Lumberjack Buying System (Outside, Inside, On the Fire, or Client)? Then write down a date by which you will have done this Next One Thing.

Remember, Sarah Golson from Chapter 3 went from $150,000 a year to $290,000 a year by simply doing the Low Hanging Fruit exercise and then tracking the "Next One Thing" on the Lumberjack Buying System.

What is the Red Flag? Ask yourself, "What, if anything, could keep me from doing the Next One Thing by the date I wrote down?" For me, it's sometimes an outside cause, but just as often, it's something in my head. It's important to write down the obstacles in your head—fear, busyness, low energy, chaos, or other progress blockers. Never run from them or try to delete them from your life. They will only rise up more powerfully. Instead, recognize them, write them down, face them, embrace them, and make them your friend. Figure out what you can learn from them and even use them to get you to the Next One Thing. Ignoring them or trying to "replace" them with positive thoughts will only make it worse.

There's lots of fun neuroscience I could throw in here, but you already know these things intuitively.

Possible Revenue. You don't need this, but it can be helpful to write down the possible revenue this Customer or Client could generate for your business in the next 12 months. It might seem small, but if you added up the 10 or 20 new Clients you intend to get this year, it could be a game changer for you.

Next Stage Date. Time kills deals. Keep people moving through the stages and record your wins here. Too often we only see success if someone becomes a Client, when really you didn't notice the great success you had moving them through all the other stages. This could also be very valuable information to help you see where you might be stalling out. At what stage in the process is that happening most (Outside Woodpile, Inside, OTF)? Now you know where to focus on improving.

The above simple spreadsheet reflects our Lumberjack Buying System analogy, which reminds us with clarity where someone is in the sales cycle and how we will know when they've been moved to the next stage. In the example above, you can only see the Outside Woodpile and Inside Woodpile. Use the link above to download the full spreadsheet.

The six "stations" for customers in the Lumberjack Buying System are:

1. **Outside Woodpile**. I can Connect and I have their data. (I might have many Connections here.)
2. **Inside Woodpile**. We have agreed to have a (Buying) Conversation.
3. **On the Fire**. I have asked the Y/N question: "Would you like to give it a try?"
4. **Client**. If the answer is Yes, great. If not, put them back in the Outside Woodpile. Never delete anyone.

5. **Advocate**. Who will refer when I ask them? They go here (Client, friend, it doesn't matter).
6. **Raving Fan**. Who refers without my asking? They go here (Client, friend, it doesn't matter).

Note that Lumberjacks (both Advocates and Raving Fans) are in what I call "The Green Zone." This is a simple but powerful reminder that your way to get off the Sales Treadmill is not by going back to the Forest to restock your Outside Woodpile with strangers but to tap into the relationships you have already built. Those people already have all the Customers or Clients you want. The best opportunities you have to grow your business revenue are in the Green Zone, not the Forest. I emphasize this as a reminder to push against the habits we were taught—to find our next customers among strangers, one at a time.

The Multiplying Power of One

In Chapter 2, I mentioned the power of Oprah Winfrey. You can sell a couple of books at a time to individual Customers at dozens of book events on a cross-country tour, or you can tap into Oprah's network and sell hundreds of thousands of copies. Every business has a potential Oprah, a Paul Bunyan Lumberjack who could turn your business on its head if you could just find them and gain their trust. These are not easy things to do, but we'll show you how they are more than just possible—they're likely.

In the first three months to a year of approaching business development this way, you may not have met an Oprah, but you may already know three to five successful business owners who know, like, and trust you—and they have all the Clients you want. Let's say you know four. Now, instead of your own list of 125 people, you have 625 potential Customers—your 125, and the 125 each of them has.

(Good Lumberjacks will often have a lot more Connections than 125, but you get my point.) Instead of relying on your list, you now have access to a much bigger Outside Woodpile than you could build in many years plugging away by yourself.

One final reminder: If you are fortunate enough to have built a lot of Connections, don't spend a lot of time creating a giant Outside Woodpile (that's Playing Office). Stop at 50 or 100, get moving on those Connections, and backfill later when you need more. I trust the next chapter will give you encouragement and a good reminder to stop planning and get moving.

My Next One Thing: The Lumberjack Buying System Report

What system or app are you using to track Connections and (Buying) Conversations? Will you use something else? What?

_____

What is your Blinding Flash of the Obvious from this chapter, and how will you apply it?

_____

Who will you share your Next One Thing with? _____

_____ When? _____

Chapter 7

WHAT'S BEHIND ME TELLS ME WHAT'S IN FRONT OF ME

Now that I'm utterly clear on cause and effect in business development, I'm really motivated to grow my business because I'm not just working hard and hoping something good happens. Because of the data behind me, I now know if I do "X." "Y" is going to happen. Clarity really is power.

—JOSH DAILEY, REAL ESTATE BROKER

The best way to drive a car is looking forward and glancing in the rear view mirror. The best way to drive a business is to look in the rear view mirror most of the time and use what you find in the past to build your future success.

—CHUCK BLAKEMAN

When I began trying to gain Utter Clarity on my First Domino, I had no data. The activity around my Three C's was something I initially decided on intuition alone. But that's a place to start, and it was much better than what I had a few minutes earlier, which was nothing. We start where we can, and as the game unfolds, we gain the Utter Clarity we're looking for.

To gain Utter Clarity on my First Domino, I developed the Leading Indicator Tracker (remember, I love Playing Office with spreadsheets). That Tracker is where I recorded my weekly Three C's activities:

- Connections
- (Buying) Conversations
- Customers/Clients

The Leading Indicator Tracker (LI Tracker) gives us Utter Clarity about how many Conversations we need each week to achieve our customer acquisition goals. You can build your own or go to 3to5Club.com/SLEMX and get the one we have used for the past couple of decades.

What Are Leading and Lagging Indicators?

For our purposes, these are two numbers that help you gain Utter Clarity on your First Domino: One number is behind you (lagging), and the other is in the future (leading), based on the number behind you. That future number, the Leading Indicator, should represent the single best activity you expect to bring you the result you want—the number of calls, texts/emails, cups of coffee, workshops, podcasts, speaking engagements, etc.

The Lagging Indicator tracks what you've already done with that singular activity. It helps you see exactly what you did last week or month, and what result you got. It's a rearview mirror. The Leading Indicator is, at first, an intuitive number we throw at the dart board that tells us if we just do a specific activity next week, we will achieve our weekly, monthly, or annual customer acquisition goals.

Once we get started, we always turn to the Lagging Indicator first to decide what activities to do in the future (the Leading Indicators of

Success). And it's our Lagging Indicator that gave me the confidence to say my First Domino was four cups of coffee per week (so I scheduled five—just in case).

Our LI Tracker is shown in Figure 7.1 below. We simply fill in the number of Connections we make each week, the number of (Buying) Conversations, and the number of new Clients/Customers. Those Three C's give us everything we need to know to understand the two most important ratios you'll ever learn in your business: your Connections to Conversations ratio, and your Conversations to Clients ratio.

Both of these can be thought of as closing ratios. In Figure 7.1, the closing ratio from Connections to Conversations is 54.05 percent, meaning that of all the people I requested to meet with and discuss business, approximately half of them have historically said yes. And one out of four of those I have met with became a Client—a closing ratio in that case of 20 percent.

I won't speak for you, but knowing these two ratios was deeply meaningful to me when I started Crankset Group, 3to5 Clubs, and a few other ventures. Nothing gets me more excited than knowing that I'm actually doing something that is nearly guaranteed to work, if I just stick with it. And I know it will work in the future (Leading Indicator) because I can look behind me and see how it has worked in the past (Lagging Indicator). The best way to drive a car is to look in front of you most of the time and glance in the rearview mirror regularly. The best way to drive a business is just the opposite: Look behind you every day, week, and month to see what has happened, and then regularly project those activities into the future—or different activities, if the past ones aren't getting the results you want. Drive your business looking in the rearview mirror. It will create a much straighter line to success than staring blankly into the future while employing the Random Hope Strategy.

	Your Closing Ratios	
# of New Clients/Lumberjacks I want each month	**4**	From your 3Cs/1st Domino Tracker Spreadsheet
Connections to Buying Conversations Ratio	41.43%	YOUR CONNECTION TO CONVERSATIONS RATIO – HOW DO YOU MAKE IT BETTER?
My Closing Ratio – Conversations to New Clients/Closings/Lumberjacks (or other result)	27.59%	YOUR CLOSING RATIO – HOW DO YOU MAKE IT BETTER?
# of WEEKLY BUYING CONVERSATIONS I need to achieve the above # of New Clients or Lumberjacks (or both) per month	3.3	You guessed at this on your 3Cs/1st Domino Spreadsheet. Now we're getting real data

Week	Week	Connections	Buying Conversations	New Clients	Closing Ratio – Connections To Conversations	Closing Ratio – Conversations To Clients
1	09/04/24	9	4	0	44.44%	0.00%
2	09/11/24	15	3	1	20.00%	33.33%
3	09/18/24	12	4	1	33.33%	25.00%

Figure 7.1: Leading/Lagging Indicators of Success

Record Your Three C's Every Week

The Leading Indicator Tracker requires you to plug in how many new Customers and/or Lumberjacks you want each month. This is the "4" that you see in green at the top of Figure 7.1. Below that, simply plug in your actual activity and results each week (Connections, Buying Conversations, and New Clients). If you download my tracker (see above), the spreadsheet formula automatically spits out closing ratios for Connections to Buying Conversations and Conversations to New Clients, along with the number of weekly Buying Conversations you need to get four new Clients each month (or however many you enter at the top of the spreadsheet).

The more weeks you input your Three C's, the more accurate the closing ratios become. You can even do this on a napkin with the calculator on your phone. I wouldn't try this right away, but if you get motivated by good data, you can eventually keep two of these trackers—one for end Customers and one for Lumberjacks. But I would encourage you to keep it simple for a while and record all Connections and Conversations in the same place. Remember, complicated things don't help us as much as we think. Make sure you really need two separate spreadsheets or separate tabs on the same spreadsheet before you go that route.

If you look back at the last week or month of Lagging Indicators and don't like what you see, that, too, is just good information. Think about what you need to adjust in next week's Leading Indicator and run at it with conviction, knowing that movement will create a better plan.

I find recording data generally unmotivating, so with rare exceptions, I keep all Connections and Conversations on simple spreadsheets like the LI Tracker. But everybody is unique. If separating potential Customers from potential Lumberjacks gives you more clarity, great. Do whatever works best for you, but make sure you record your Three C's faithfully, so you can know your First Domino with certainty, *the most important business number you will ever have.* In this case, recording your Lagging and Leading Indicators is both simple and easy, so you have no excuses for not knowing your First Domino. Clarity is power, and Utter Clarity is as powerful as it gets.

Remember the "annoying" question my wife Diane would ask about how next month is shaping up? The Leading Indicator spreadsheet gave me the data I needed to answer it with confidence. If the worst of human conditions is uncertainty, you won't have to worry about it in your business development, once you find your First Domino and commit to moving on it.

First Domino Clarity Is Motivating

At one point around 2006-2007, while I was building Crankset Group, I had something like 16 straight Buying Conversations over four weeks where nobody bought anything, and I was beginning to worry that something was wrong with me. Worse yet, after almost a year, I was wondering if maybe I was down a rabbit hole with a business idea that wasn't going to work. So I took a walk and asked myself one of my favorite soul-searching questions, "What am I pretending not to know?" It's always good to start with what I might be able to adjust inside me before looking for problems "out there."

But equally important was my ability to look at the data. Without my LI Tracker, all I would have had to rely on would be four weeks of anecdotal experience with no context. It just felt like "this" was not going to work, and I had weeks of experiential data to "prove" it. But as I looked back over almost a year of LI Tracker data, I saw that, while there were lots of ups and downs, the general trend showed that if I just kept going, I would break even in 18 to 24 months, instead of the 12 months my initial spreadsheet had indicated. Diane and I talked and decided we could loan ourselves another 6 to 12 months, and I resolved to keep having Buying Conversations over coffee.

And the law of averages kicked in. Almost everyone I talked to in the next two weeks became a Client, and I was right back to my closing ratio of about one in four Buying Conversations resulting in a Client. Had I not had those objective Lagging Indicators to review, it would have been much harder to keep going. Our brains are much more inclined to pay attention to recent events, and in my case, they were nothing but discouraging. The LI Tracker put me back on course, and we have Crankset Group business advisors and 3to5 Clubs (business owner masterminds) on three continents as a result.

Around the sixth week of aggressively and intentionally working on her Three C's, Elvi Bjorg, owner of a marketing company, reported, "I feel like I'm drowning in coffee. I've got like 20 people to talk to and I don't know where I'm going to find the time. I'm a little tired, and I don't have a single sale yet." Elvi's experience is not unusual. We looked at her Lagging Indicators, and she was quickly reminded that six weeks ago she didn't have a single potential prospect, and virtually no one to talk to. Drowning in coffee was a huge step forward. And as we shared at the very beginning of this book, she quadrupled her income within a few more weeks.

My LI Tracker has allowed me to be resilient and strong, full of grit and fortitude—all valuable if reactionary responses to trouble that comes and finds us. But more important, it helped me be relentless, which is forward-moving and doesn't wait around for trouble to appear. "Relentless" pushes forward, actively creating its own trouble, like a stream running downhill. We'll have much more on being relentless later in the book. But for now, remember that your LI Tracker and your First Domino will be among the most supportive "partners" you will ever have to help you proactively build a great business and a fulfilling life.

Keep going.

My Next One Thing: Leading and Lagging Indicators of Success

How are you tracking your two Leading and Lagging Indicators of Success?

_____

_____

_____

What is your most reliable **Lagging** Indicator of Success? It is either a specific type and number of Connections you make every week (phone, email, events, seminars, webinars, podcasts, etc.) or the number of (Buying) Conversations you have every week.

_____

How does that Lagging Indicator help you form your **Leading** Indicator of Success for next week/next month?

_____

What is your Blinding Flash of the Obvious from this chapter, and how will you apply it?

_____

Who will you share your Next One Thing with? _____

_____ When? _____

Chapter 8

FOUR QUESTIONS THAT CHANGE EVERYTHING

*I had 2,200 wealth management Clients when I first learned
the principles in this book. I learned the Four Walking-In
Commitments and the Four Buying Questions and used them to
build relationships instead of stabbing people with my business
card. I now have less than two dozen Clients and make eight times
what I used to make by chasing strangers. I've taken FasTrak eight
times because it has been so valuable to me in building a great
business and gaining Freedom in my business, not from it.*

—Jason Deringer, wealth manager

Be interested, not interesting. You'll be more successful.

—Chuck Blakeman

Who's in charge of a conversation—the person talking, or the
person asking questions? Communication experts will tell
you it's the person asking questions. This isn't always a controlling
mechanism, of course. It can be a guiding mechanism. You want to
guide the other person into a full understanding of how your product
or service can help, and more important, you want to guide them to a
deep trust of you. Remember, nobody wants to be sold anything, but

everybody wants to buy. The Four Walking-In Commitments and the Four Buying Questions will create that dynamic of curiosity and leaning into what you have to offer.

Before we start, however, here are three Buying Principles that have served me well over the years in flipping the script from me selling to them buying:

1. **Meet them where they are, not where you want them to be.** Many sales tactics are built around luring the potential Customer to "join me over here," mentally or emotionally, for a great look at my product from *my* point of view. When we do the opposite and meet them where *they* are, we gain their trust. Where are they right now, personally or in business? The Four Buying Questions will help answer that later in this chapter.

2. **Seek to understand, not to be understood** (with acknowledgment to Stephen Covey). Listen and truly hear what they have to say first and listen more than you talk. If you want them to understand you, they need to know you understand them first.

3. **Serve; don't sell.** Their best interest must be served, even if it means sending them to someone else when your product isn't what they need. Many times, what people want is not what they need, and selling them what they want could backfire on you, and on them.

The Four Walking-In Commitments

With these three simple Buying Principles in mind, over the years I also got in the habit of reviewing four intentions we call Walking-In Commitments before each meeting with a potential Client. Those intentions reinforce the powerful "serve; don't sell" mindset. I memorized them and review them every time:

1. I intend to serve this person, not to sell.
2. I will not talk about my business unless asked.
3. I intend to make money from this meeting.
4. I will make an offer.

At first, you might see some conflicts between those four commitments. It could easily look like committing to a couple of them would make it impossible to commit to the other two. So let's unpack this.

I intend to serve, not sell. Nobody wants to be sold anything. I intend to find out what they need and offer them that, even if it's somebody else's product or service. I'm committed to doing what is best for them, not for our company. If both interests line up, that's great. If not, I will steer them to a product or service that truly meets their needs.

I will not talk about my business unless asked. This sounds like financial suicide, right? But I've been committed to it for a few decades, and I'm convinced you will make more money this way. And really, if you sit with them over a cup of coffee for 45 to 60 minutes and they never ask about your business, do you really want to do business with them?

I intend to make money from this meeting. If I just want to serve, and I won't talk about my business unless asked, it might be hard to see how I'm going to make money from this meeting. Please note, though, I didn't say I would make money *in* this meeting—but I intend to make money *from* it. I once met with a business owner and found out in the first few minutes that it was her 20th anniversary, and she and her spouse had lost their babysitter for that evening. Did she need my business services right then? So, in the spirit of serving, not selling, I knew this was not the time to launch into who my business could help her.

I intend to make an offer. No matter the circumstance, you can almost always make an offer, even if it isn't related to your business. And sometimes those are the better, more powerful offers. In that moment she didn't need me to launch into how we could help her business. If I truly intended to serve her, than my offer should reflect that. Remember, we need to meet people where they are, not where we want them to be. She needed a babysitter. So I got hold of my wife and got some contacts, and we called around until we found a babysitter. That took 20 minutes or so, and we didn't have much time left for a Buying Conversation. I offered to meet again, but we never managed it. And yet I still intended to make money from that and every other meeting. And I did.

Six or eight months later, a different owner called who needed business advice on her rapidly growing company. She signed up with me, and we enjoyed a great working relationship for a long time. This owner was the sister of the woman who had lost her babysitter—and that's how I kept all four Walking-In Commitments. I served the first business owner by finding her a babysitter, I didn't talk about my business because it didn't come up in the context of solving her problem. I gave her an offer (a babysitter), and many months later I made money *from* that one-time meeting by signing on her sister as a Client. You don't have to see this as some kind of mystical karma. You get what you intend, and you reap what you sow. Or, if you prefer, the more you intend, the more you achieve.

The Four Walking-In Commitments separate you from all the other salespeople who have been taught the only successful conclusion to a meeting is to sell you their product or service. It is my conviction that when we develop *relationships* instead of transactions, we will always do better in the long run. I would love it if everybody who came in needed my services. But there's a better way to succeed. I recommend you memorize these Walking-In Commitments along with the following Four Buying Questions.

The Four Buying Questions

We developed the Four Buying Questions over the course of many years. I now use them reflexively with most potential Clients and even with guests at a dinner party to show interest and be others centered. As I mentioned above, the Four Buying Questions flip the script from me having to sell to them wanting to buy. This is because the questions are designed to help them, not help me. In the process, I will discover things that help me relate the value of my service to their needs, not mine. But it's not about finding their "pain" point. It's just about listening and caring.

The Four Buying Questions are designed to help them, not you. And that's OK because you'll get what you need by being interested in them. The exact wording can vary, but they should focus on four areas: past, present, future, and ideal Customer.

1. **Past.** In a B2B conversation, you might ask, "What made you want to get into this business?" Or, in a B2C conversation, a realtor might ask a homeowner, "What was your favorite place you ever lived, and what did you like most about it?"
2. **Future.** "It's been great hearing why you got into this business/what your favorite home was. So where's it all taking you? What's your end game?"
3. **Present.** "If that's your end game, what's the one thing most standing in your way right now that might keep you from getting there?"
4. Describe your **ideal Customer/Client**. I'd love to see if I know anyone like that.

Let's look a little deeper into why the Four Buying Questions flip the script and make them want to buy.

Past. How does the "Past" question serve them? It's very likely they have forgotten why they originally got into business or where their favorite place was that they once lived. Asking will help remind them that their business was supposed to be fun, or that their next house should reflect what they loved about that favorite place. Don't just move on right away to the next question—that could feel like an interrogation. Be prepared to answer the question briefly yourself. That will help them get to know you and keep them from feeling like they're being cross-examined.

Future. Over the years, I have observed that very few people have given much thought to what they want in the long run. It is helpful if you can get them to describe some future that works for them, whether it has to do with their business, their next house, their financial portfolio, etc.

An important aside: Often when I ask a business owner what their end game is, they give me a business-speak answer, like raise revenues and profits, increase market share, etc. I wait for them to finish or gently interrupt, and then apologize. "I'm sorry, I wasn't clear. I mean what is your *personal* end game? What do you want out of this business?" I find people usually aren't thinking of themselves, which is why I ask broadly, "What is your end game?" That lets them interpret and answer the question however they want, whether personally or in terms of business success. Sometimes it can be a gentle but powerful wake-up call that they've forgotten about themselves while building their business. Success, after all, is not measured by how impressive our businesses are, but by how well they support us in leading a fulfilling and rich personal life.

Present. I went through my first five businesses without connecting with my personal end game, so I never thought about what would stand in the way of my reaching my own end game, which has always been freedom *in* my business, not *from* it. What if they walked away from your meeting with clarity about hiring someone, changing products, sourcing somewhere else, raising their prices, or moving someone along who would be a better fit elsewhere? What a valuable cup of coffee that would be. Priceless, really.

Ideal Customer. Most often, before I get to the fourth question, the other person will begin asking questions back to me, usually about my business, even if it's just why or how I got into it. At that point, I feel I have permission to talk about my business. And if we've made it through two or three of the Buying Questions, I probably have discovered one or two things from their past, future, and/or present that I can connect with how my product or service could help them.

Meet Them Where They Are, Not Where You Want Them to Be

The Four Buying Questions can reduce any 45-minute sales spiel to about five minutes. Most of us have a long pitch ready because we didn't bother to find out what they really need first. So we drone away, boring them with our entire presentation quiver of arrows, just in case one of the "features and benefits" will strike a chord. But if you take the time to listen and understand their needs, you'll know the one or two things you really need to address, and you can just pull those couple of things out and talk about how you can meet their need, not how you can sell stuff.

It's an amazing moment when you can stop selling because they want to buy. When you are curious about people, most buyers will see that you're not trying to sell. You just make them *aware* of what you have to offer. You're no longer persuading—you're just engaging with them to create awareness. And in that context, if the product or service is something they need, people are much more likely to lean in with a desire to buy.

Once they ask, you can tell them all about your great chair: how you source the wood sustainably, make your own glue, etc. Until then, keep all that in your pocket. If they never ask, there are two likely reasons. First, they may not be interested in other people, in which case I'm personally less motivated to do business with them. Or second, they have something very distracting going on in their lives. If that's the case, you should be able to detect that as you listen to them. I'll always suggest another meeting (or help them with their distraction right there if I can). If, on the other hand, they're simply not interested in you or your service, consider it a victory that you found out before you brought them on as a (likely difficult) Client.

We seek first to understand, then to be understood, which is Stephen Covey's version of "serve; don't sell." I once worked with a great business coach in Richmond, Virginia, who had a truly amazing presentation and a lot of really good ways to help people. But he was having trouble bringing people across the finish line.

I suggested that for a couple of weeks he might start with the Four Buying Questions before presenting anything, and then tailor his presentation to what either their pain point or, more critically, their "Joy Point" was. He came back two weeks later and said, "I'm a genius. I just asked a few questions, listened, and then shared back what I heard them say they wanted. I focused on their Joy Point. And they would say things like, 'That's exactly what I want. I would love to see that happen in my business.' How did you know?" His close rate went up exponentially when he focused on serving instead of selling, and on their Joy Point instead of their pain point. (I'll talk more about Joy Points a little later in this chapter.)

I Just Lost Control

If you meet someone with high social awareness and high empathy, they're likely going to say hello and start asking you questions before you get a chance to say anything. I love it when I find someone like that, and I always want to honor their genuine curiosity. But I also want to make sure we have our Buying Conversation, not "just" a really great time connecting as human beings. So while we're saying hello and before we order coffee, I try to say something like, "Tom, really great to meet you. Sarah has said a lot of good things about you, and I'm really looking forward to finding out more about you and your business."

Then you can both drift off into some basic get-to-know-you talk (where you live, where you're from, the weather, etc.). But by the time you sit down, it would be great to start diving into the Four Buying Questions. If they jump the gun and ask you about your business, you can thank them and then remind them laughingly, "I appreciate you asking, but I asked you first when we were getting coffee. I'll jump in as well, but I'd love to hear first how you got into the business you own now (or what was your favorite house, or whatever Past question would work for your product or service)." If that doesn't distract them from their question, you can answer briefly and then jump in with your first Buying Question. It's a dance—you'll learn it just by doing it a few times. And remember—don't talk about your business unless you're asked. You'll make more money and have more fun with people you love being around.

Find Their Joy Point

Here's another not-great idea sales courses have been touting for a century—find the potential customer's pain point, and tell them how your product can solve their pain. I suggest you do the opposite— find their Joy Point. Sometimes you have to hear their pain point to guide them to their Joy Point, but usually in their answers to the Four Buying Questions, you will find something that just lights them up in the Past or Future, and even sometimes in the Present.

Neuroscience teaches us that when we focus on eliminating pain, it doesn't usually work—sometimes we end up with even more pain. I have found that when I ran away from hard things or tried to just push them out, I ended up dealing with them later. I had to learn to embrace and work through them. We are much more motivated to run toward something we love than away from something we hate or fear. Help them run toward their Joy Point, not away from their pain point. Many times you can actually solve the pain point in the process. This one tip alone could double your income in 90 days.

Make an Offer

A famous line from the David Mamet play about salespeople, *Glengarry Glen Ross*, is "A-B-C. A, always; B, be; C, closing. Always be closing!" It's a bit harsh and transactional for me, but the sentiment is good. We're not having this coffee just to ask them the Four Buying Questions because they will enjoy it. If you don't acquire Customers, you won't be having any more of these great conversations. So always make an offer, which could be offering them your product or service ("Would you like to give it a try?") or offering to meet again to continue the conversation, or offering to help them find a babysitter.

Never Ask Directly for a Referral

That's right. Stop it. Yes, I know I asked you to find Lumberjacks who will refer to you. And the best way to do that is not to ask for a referral in the traditional sense, but to do it indirectly. There's a better way to get potential Lumberjacks to open their Outside Woodpiles to you. The classic referral request—"Do you know anybody you could refer me to?"—is justifiably full of psychological roadblocks. Here's how to indirectly ask for a referral that instead asks them to be a help to their friends. And who doesn't want to help their friends?

*Do you know one other person who might
benefit from the experience you're having?*

We have fine-tuned every word in this question over many years. Here's what goes on in slow motion in their mind and heart as they hear the question:

Do you know . . .	(Well, I have to know something, of course I know.)
. . . one other person . . .	(I can't be that lonely, of course I know one other person!)
. . . who might benefit . . .	(Good reminder. This guy didn't try to sell me, he just asked great questions, found my Joy Point, and helped me where I needed it. He's not going to pressure any of my friends either.)
. . . from the experience you're having?	(I can see how beneficial this will be for me. That's why I signed on the dotted line. Why wouldn't I want to help my friends have the same good experience?)

When we ask for three classic "do you know anybody" referrals, we usually get none—it creates chaos in the person's head, who is trying to think of multiple people at once. But if we ask for *one*, we might just get three, because they easily found one, and, well, there's another right beside the first one. And when we ask them to help their friends instead of use them, the desire to refer goes up significantly.

Research and my own anecdotal experience say there are at least four great times to ask someone to refer an end Client or a Lumberjack:

1. **As soon as they sign on with you as a Client.** The benefits of doing so are the freshest they will ever be, and sharing the opportunity with their friends helps them validate their decision.

2. **Right after you heroically fix a screw-up.** When I bring on Clients, I often tell them that because we're not perfect, it's pretty much a given that we will disappoint them somewhere along the road. "So I'm not going to tell you we won't ever mess up," I say. "Just the opposite—we're guaranteed to do so. And when we do, you will see just how well we can fix the situation. That will separate us from others you could have signed up with, who will also disappoint you at some time." So, a great time to ask them to bless their friend is just after you have heroically fixed an error. However, if they don't see you've done an amazing job of fixing the error, then it's not going to be a good time to ask.

3. **When they're leaving you.** Most products or services have a half-life, and if you've served this person well, they will be glad to send you others. We have had past Clients send us future Clients for years after we parted ways.

4. **Just about any other time.** Again, if all you're doing is asking them to help their friends, there simply isn't a bad time to do that.

These three tools—the Four Walking-In Commitments, the Four Buying Questions, and the Non-Referral Question—have been live-tested for many years. I strongly encourage you to memorize and use them to guide your meetings with potential Clients, as well as what you want out of events and meetings you go to.

My Next One Thing: Walking-In Commitments and the Four Buying Questions

How will you use the Walking-In Commitments and the Four Buying Questions going forward?

_____

How will you identify your potential Customers' Joy Points going forward?

_____

What is your Blinding Flash of the Obvious from this chapter, and how will you apply it?

_____

Who will you share your Next One Thing with? _____

_____ When? _____

Chapter 9

TIER THREE LISTENING

Everyone said I had a great service, but I wasn't closing sales. I learned Tier Three Listening, started putting together proposals from that place, and sales doubled right away. People thought I was a genius, and all I did was learn how to actively listen.

—JIM ROGAN, CEO COACHING, INC.

Love always seeks the long-term best interest of the one being loved. All successful businesses are founded on love. Love is motivated by adding value, not extracting it.

—CHUCK BLAKEMAN

What we'll talk about in this chapter is, in my opinion, about the most important, most challenging listening practice most of us will ever learn: Tier Three Listening.

I will invest the rest of my life in continuing to learn this skill. We don't come by it naturally, and it's not ours just because we have a lot of years behind us. It will not help us "survive" individually—in fact, it uniquely places how I'm doing and what I'm feeling right now on the shelf for a brief moment, which makes me as vulnerable as I could ever be. But that also creates deep openness to what others are thinking, feeling, and wanting, without regard to how all that might help (or hurt) me. And that vulnerability is the source of untold power to lead, build relationships, and attract Customers in ways most of us have rarely experienced. And it's magic when it happens.

Many years ago, I worked with a brilliant leadership consultant who had a great contribution to make but was struggling to land Clients. He built great, detailed, logical, and powerful proposals and was a master at presenting them. At the time, I hadn't really figured anything of this system out, but I did know that if you want something to change, you have to change something. I asked him to go into his first meeting and simply ask a few questions, something like the following, and then just listen:

- What do you want, and by when? (Goal)
- What do you need in order to get it? (Resources)
- What could stand in your way? (Obstacle)
- How could you solve it? (Solution)
- What do you think you should do first? (The Next One Thing)

And after listening to the answers, I suggested he simply share back with them, "This is what I think I heard . . . did I get that right?" And then he could build a proposal specifically, and only, around that. I was winging it, but what he was doing wasn't working, so he needed to try something new.

We met two weeks later, and he was ecstatic. He said he had tried the above tactic with four people and already had two new Clients as a result. And the most surprising thing to him was that after he gave them the feedback, they were telling him how spot-on he was. They also wondered how he knew so clearly what they needed and asked, "When can we start?" He laughed and said, "I didn't come up with any of it. I just fed back what I heard." The questions he asked were more specific to coaching or advisory work, so over the next couple of years, we went on to develop the Four Buying Questions to flip the script from us needing to sell to them wanting to buy. But one thing remained constant—asking questions and listening is at the core.

So many people in the past 50 years have focused on the relationship-building power of listening. Stephen Covey made it one of his Seven Habits of Highly Successful People in his book of the same name and said, "Seek first to understand, then to be understood." And countless studies have shown us what listening does to build trust, confidence, and an ever-deepening relationship.

Remember, nobody wants to be sold anything, but everyone wants to buy. So how do we get to where we're no longer selling but they are proactively pursuing us to buy? Tier Three Listening is a skill we use in combination with the Four Walking-In Commitments and the Four Buying Questions to flip that script. When we're asking those questions and listening at the highest level, the results can be very dramatic. This is a core skill in continuing to apply the core principle of *Sell Less, Earn More, to* serve; not sell.

Needs vs Wants

An important part of gaining people's confidence is hearing them, especially hearing what they want. Too often, we are so excited about our offering that we start presenting what we think they *need*, before we ever find out what they *want* (or what they *really* need). This is what was holding back my consultant friend above.

Tier Three Listening allows us to find out what they really, truly want before we ever propose what they might need. We will never get them to embrace what they need if they don't first have full confidence that we understand what they want. When people understand that I have heard them, and I can share back with empathy what I understand they want, only then might they be open to hearing about other things they could need. Sharing with someone what they might actually need too soon risks the relationship if they are not ready to hear it. But when we hear what they want and share that back with them, we have a shot at moving them to what they need, if it is different from what they want. And if it's the same, all the better. You can very quickly show them how what you have to offer meets both their desire *and* their need.

A World of Abundance

Remember, you either live in a world of abundance or in a world of scarcity, and whichever one you choose affects every decision you make. Choose abundance. If what you have to offer is what they want but is not, in your best estimate, what they actually need, don't sell it to them. Even if they persist. The implications of doing so go far beyond this one-time mistake.

One of my best Lumberjacks ever was a mortgage broker. In the few years before the Great Recession of 2008-2009, the entire mortgage industry was offering what they generously called "stated income loans," which became cynically known as "liar's loans." Just tell me what you make, and I'll give you a loan based on what you said, no income verification required. My friend gently and steadfastly refused to do these loans. She always required verification.

People who didn't want to verify would ask her for a referral to another mortgage company, and she politely wouldn't do it. One of the rare moments we should not refer is when it is not in the best interests of the Client. If you don't have what they want, you should refer, unless there simply isn't another option you can see that would serve them. And in this case, my friend was deeply convinced that stated income loans did not benefit anyone but the mortgage companies selling them. Years after the housing crash and millions of foreclosures nationwide, she had many people thank her for selling them what they needed, not what they wanted, and others who shared that they wished they had listened to her.

Other times it isn't in people's best interests to buy from us, even when they are primed to do so. The simple principle that applies for me at all times in business development is that I will always do what is in the long-term best interest of the potential Customer. And if buying from me is not to their long-term advantage, I need to pass, no matter how much they want to buy from me. It's another great reason to have Lumberjacks in your profession to whom you can refer people when they are a low-percentage match to your solution and a high-percentage match to someone else's. It will come back to you later because you did what Zig Ziglar encouraged: You helped others get what they needed first.

Love in Business

I firmly believe all good businesses run on love. No exceptions. I describe love the following way:

Love always seeks the long-term best interests of the one being loved.

If that describes love, it also describes good business, good marketing, and good sales. Cheap marketing and self-focused sales do not consider whether their product is best for someone—they just want the sale. If you buy something that isn't a good fit, even if I know that when I sell it to you, that's on you. You made the decision, you signed the papers, and too bad, so sad if you later find out there was a much better way to go. If I'm not operating out of love, my job isn't to help you get what you need—my job is to sell whatever I can.

Great business always seeks the long-term best interests of their Customers. It's how you create great lifetime value for them. There are two kinds of profit—Good Profit and Bad Profit. Bad Profit always looks for the short-term gain. Selling $9.00 gas cans at $45.00 after a hurricane is Bad Profit. Selling someone something they don't really need is also Bad Profit. Any sale that might later leave a bad taste in someone's mouth after they figure out they've been hoodwinked or oversold is Bad Profit. If you go for Bad Profit, you will find yourself in a lifetime of one-time sales, always chasing one stranger after another. People who know you will be crossing the street to avoid you. But Good Profit creates loyal Customers.

As an important aside here, I would add that confusing pricing is also Bad Profit. I had a CEO once whose mantra was, "Where there is confusion, there is profit." The airlines have been masters of confusion for years with all their add-on costs and variable pricing. The government had to pass a law to get mortgage brokers and credit card companies to reveal what the actual costs are. Much of the merchant credit processing industry (the guys that collect the 2.5 percent or so fee from merchants who accept credit cards) has always operated under a "you'll never figure out the actual cost" premise. We found one that didn't operate that way, and we refer them all the time. Don't sell for any company where confusion is part of their path to profit. It is never in the long-term best interests of the Customer.

Love your spouse. Love your kids. Love your dog. Love the world around you. And do so by seeking everything and everyone's long-term best interests, including your Customers'. They are people, too, and listening to them share their stories and dreams helps create trusting relationships better than anything else we can do. Trust is the number-one asset of any relationship, and when we have trust, the buying floodgates open. Listening makes people feel loved and opens those floodgates.

I'm not a naturally good listener. It has taken a lot of conscious effort and will be something I work on for the rest of my life. In the process, I'm grasping some simple principles around listening. A real Blinding Flash of the Obvious (BFO)[7] for me was learning that if someone asked me questions and I was doing all the talking, I wasn't in control of the conversation, even though the other person couldn't get a word in edgewise.

Who's in charge of a conversation? That's the person asking the questions, not the person talking. And as long as I have their best interests at heart, moving the conversation in a direction that serves them, not me, is a great reason to be in control. And don't worry—if they're interested in building a relationship, they'll turn the tables and start asking about you. If they're not, you probably don't want to do business with them anyway. Let's look at the three levels or "Tiers" of listening, with each described and identified with a simple question we ask ourselves at each level.

Tier One Listening

Tier One Listening asks, "How do *I* think and feel about *me*?"

It is a very important skill. Recent neurological research tells us our response to any stimulus happens first in our bodies, then goes to the emotional part of the brain, which sends it over to the cognitive part to decide whether we should actually be tense right now. Tier One Listening is a critical foundation for communication because if we are not good at interpreting our own bodily responses and emotions, we are significantly hampered in our ability to read anybody else's.

When do we begin to develop Tier One Listening skills? I would think we're already doing it before we're born, but certainly from birth on. We are very aware of being in a strange new, very bright, very loud, very cold world. And we are extremely good at expressing

---

7   I originally learned this term from Art Radtke and continue to use it to close almost every meeting as we go around and share what we've learned. So much of life is intuitive or things we already know—we just need a reminder from time to time.

our Tier One Listening skills by crying for food, warmth, and desire for human touch. Early on, it's all about Tier One Listening—it's all about me. And that's appropriate. Learning about me helps me discover how to learn about you.

I personally believe that we already have a lot of Tier One Listening ability at birth, but sadly many of us, especially men, lose much of it very early on. We're taught not to pay attention to our inner selves: stop showing emotion, stop crying, buck up, and move on. And even many therapy modalities still teach us to react to what's going on in our bodies and emotions as the enemy that needs to be purged and chased away.

In the late 20th century, coaching was only for the broken employee. Now it's seen as just as important for those who represent the future leadership of the company. It's not just for fixing broken parts, but also for getting exponentially better in areas where we might already exhibit proficiency. The sooner we normalize emotional therapy (not just cognitive) for "healthy" people (whatever that means), the better. As a recovered rugged individualist, I have benefited a great deal from attention to inner work. It's the basis for the outer work, including being a great business development person. The better I am at feeling what is going on inside me, and why I view the world the way I do, the more available I will be to do the same with Customers. Tier One Listening is our gateway.

A good therapist can teach you to embrace everything going on inside so you can repurpose it and grow new emotional "muscles" to become better at attracting new Customers. I have benefited for many years now from people I refer to as "rent-a-friends," who have been Outside Eyes to my life. People are surprised when they learn I've been in ongoing individual, couples, and group therapy, because obviously only wounded people go to therapy, and I don't come across as wounded. The dirty little secret is, no matter how good we are at putting on our public persona, we all have wounded parts from childhood that could benefit deeply from Outside Eyes. Vulnerability is the foundation of power.

Therapy isn't the only way or maybe even the easiest way to learn Tier One Listening—it's just the fastest. Asking yourself the question at the beginning of this section every morning and focusing on expressing a feeling attached to the moment is a great way to get started. Having a safe person to share that with every morning is even better.

I used to think we could feel just a few emotions; anger, sadness, happiness, fear, and maybe a couple more. Did you know there are well over 100 emotions we cycle through on an almost daily basis? The Emotion Grid, developed by Marc Brackett in his book *Permission to Feel*, shows 100 separate emotions on the grid. And that's not exhaustive. Marc's grid is just one of many such "mood meters," but I like his because it creates four quadrants that help sort our feelings.[8]

If you're good at sensing how your body reacts and your emotions engage, that's a great first step. If you've been taught, as I was, to not sense your body or feel your emotions, relearning this natural but suppressed skill is a great place to start to build your Steady Stream of Potential Clients.

Tier Two Listening

Tier Two Listening asks, "How do *others* think and feel about *me*?"

This is a basic survival skill. If I'm not aware of threats to my life, I'm not going to make it long. And on a sliding scale, there are always threats and opportunities I will miss if I'm not tuned in to the signals others are sending about me. A lot of great Client acquisition has been lost by not practicing Tier Two Listening and,

---

8   Marc Brackett, *Permission to Feel* (Celadon Books). You can see his Emotion Grid at thewell.world/files/resources/permission.pdf.

as a result, missing things that were said, or unsaid, or expressed in their posture and facial expressions.

Some neurologists say that something like 60 percent to 90 percent of what we communicate is nonverbal—we say it with our bodies, facial expressions, and tone of voice. If you're not practicing Tier Two Listening, you're likely to have a tough time getting people to the point where they want to buy. Tier Two needs the same Outside Eyes as Tier One, even if it's just a great friend who will speak with grace, love, and kindness about the blind spots in your understanding of how others view you.

Tier One and Two = Emotional Intelligence

I personally believe Tier One and Tier Two combine to form what we call "emotional intelligence." An emotionally intelligent person will not just know what they are thinking and feeling, but they will also have tools in place to manage their responses to those thoughts and emotions. They are good at knowing what others think and feel about them, and they know how to manage their responses to that as well. Knowing how we and others feel about us is only half the equation—the "awareness" part. Knowing how to run toward, embrace, learn from, and coparent our "parts" that are getting in the way is the other half. That is the "management" part of emotional intelligence, and it takes a lifetime, which is part of the fun of living.

Why spend so much time on this in a book about customer acquisition? Because the facts are compelling:[9]

- Emotional intelligence (EI) determines 58 percent of success. All other factors or skills account for only 42 percent.

---

9   *Emotional Intelligence 2.0* by Travis Bradberry and Jean Greaves (TalentSmart, $14.98).

- Ninety percent of top performers have it, and 90 percent of bottom performers don't.
- Salespeople with *average* EI outperform those with the *highest* IQs *70 percent of the time.*
- Salespeople with *average* EI outperform those with *average* IQs *80 percent of the time.*
- You make more money.
- You are happier.

We could all benefit from doing work on our Tier One and Tier Two Listening skills (see Figure 9.1 below). They are foundational to our success, both in business and in life. People run toward those who are good at them. And we live with more joy in the process.

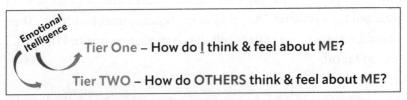

Figure 9.1: Tier One and Tier Two Listening—Emotional Intelligence

The joy is in knowing that the more we learn to be aware of and able to manage those embodied thoughts and feelings, the more we will enjoy life, enjoy other people, and be better available to serve without selling. In the process, we will sell more, faster. I could quote multiple studies over decades that show emphatically that someone with average emotional intelligence makes more money, does better in life, and is happier than someone with a high IQ. If I want to be fulfilled and successful, emotional intelligence trumps IQ every time.

Tier Three Listening

Tier Three Listening asks, "How do *others* think and feel about *themselves*, and *how do I enter into that*?"

Notice I said "enter into." It's not how do I solve it, or even how do I support the other person, but how do I simply come alongside and try to understand what they're thinking about themselves? You don't have to actually understand them. You simply have to try to understand, and you're in Tier Three.

For many years, I thought Tiers One and Two were all there was in sales, and that Tier Two Listening in particular was the key to great sales. I used to think that what we really need to know is what others are thinking and feeling about *us*. Knowing that, I could bludgeon people with my long list of features and benefits while I watched for a positive "hit" that made them connect with me. Then I could just focus on expanding the conversation around that hit. I was so far off.

The Golden Heart Award

Tier Three Listening changes everything. It is the purview of those who have cracked the code of great customer acquisition and great relationships in general. Tiers One and Two describe emotional intelligence, whereas Tier Three is all about empathy and compassion,[10] which is very different (see Figure 9.2 below). And through this third level of listening, we can see our sales go through the roof. I experienced this, and it has also been the experience of countless business development people who have cracked the

---

10 I describe "empathy" as feeling what others feel and "compassion" as taking action to support someone. Both in combination have been very helpful to me in connecting with existing and potential customers.

Tier Three Listening code, including the consultant quoted at the beginning of this chapter. Tier Three Listening is *the* game changer, the Golden Heart of great business development.

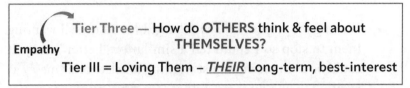

Figure 9.2: Tier Three Listening—Empathy

I believe this is the most adult listening skill, and many people never develop it to any effective degree. It's not a survival skill; in fact, it can be seen as a threat to survival. To fully enter into someone else's thinking and feeling, I have to recognize and then put aside how I'm feeling about me. I even have to disregard how they're feeling about me. This is not something we do organically or instinctively. Empathy and compassion require deliberate and intentional practice in getting outside myself and alongside someone else.

Tier Three Listening requires me to be fully invested in what the other person is thinking and feeling and how I can simply be with them in that moment. Yes, it could grow into supporting them, talking, or even offering solutions, but my experience is that it starts with just relating, understanding, and investing my energy in thinking about what it's like to be them right now, thinking what they're thinking and feeling what they're feeling.

Empathy and compassion are at a very different level than emotional intelligence. When I first began to intentionally practice Tier Three, I was very surprised to realize I spent very little time there, maybe less than 5 percent of my "listening" time with people. I have since come a long way in developing it. You can, too. We're never done learning and growing.

AM I TIER THREE?

How do you know if you're not in Tier Three? After discovering this Tier, over a few months I identified some indicators that I was still in Tier One or Two:

- *Waiting for people to finish talking.* I found myself wanting them to stop so I could tell a similar or "better" story. It could be as innocent as just wanting to relate or as messy as wanting to one-up them. Either way, developing a response while they're talking and waiting for them to pause for breath is just another form of interrupting people. Sadly, I was really good at this, and I still am. We're always growing.
- *Distracted.* Squirrel! Looking around the room, noticing movement in the background, scanning for a friend you're expecting . . . my ADHD would kick in often. I have trained myself to listen better and be much less ADHD in those circumstances. It's doable. When you recognize you're in Tier One or Two, ask yourself the Tier Three question to help refocus on them.
- *Mental wandering.* In this case, I'm not distracted by things in the room, but by things in my head; a sourdough recipe, my workout this morning, things on my to-do list . . .
- *Asking yes/no.* Yes/no questions just set me up to keep talking. When I ask exploratory questions instead, I'm inviting them to share as deeply and in whatever direction they want to go. "Do you prefer orange or blue?" (a form of Yes/No question because it gives you only two choices) becomes "What's your favorite color and what draws you to it?" "Did you like the lecture she gave?" becomes "How did you feel about the lecture she gave?"
- *Next-level questions.* Getting an answer to one question makes me want to find out more. This is one of the best ways for you to know you're in Tier Three and for someone to feel you're really listening to them. You heard something they said that made you want to ask something else. That's deep listening.

TIER THREE—THE COURAGE TO SERVE

There have been many times that using Tier Three Listening, combined with the Four Buying Questions, has shown me that the potential Client either wants something they don't need or needs something I can't provide. This is a good time to remember a couple of valuable principles I shared with you before:

1. Love always seeks the long-term best interests of the one being loved. Love doesn't serve my own short-term interests. I choose love.
2. We either live in a world of abundance or in a world of scarcity, and whichever one we choose affects every decision we make. I choose abundance.

THEIR LONG-TERM BEST INTERESTS

One of the amazing things about going fully Tier Three with someone is that it frees us to share what we feel would be the best solution for them, without regard for how they might react. I'm not motivated by Tier One (what I'm feeling about me) or even Tier Two (what they are feeling about me). I'm fully focused on what is in their long-term best interests and can freely share that without fear of them disliking me. Instead of worrying, "Will they like me for presenting what they need instead of what they want?", the question becomes, "Am I willing to love them even if, for a moment, they don't like me?"

That's true Tier Three Listening. By building this trust, you now have permission to do what is best for them, even if that means risking your relationship. Choose to be both kind and direct. Get outside yourself, come alongside them, meet their need, and watch them light up.

We use Tier Three Listening to help us understand their responses to the time-tested and highly effective Four Buying Questions we shared in Chapter 8. When asking these questions and listening at this level, we are much more likely to find out both what others want and what they need (which could be the same or completely different). And then the fun begins. We are now in a position to truly serve them with how we respond. I call this the process of bringing Clarity, Hope, and Risk to our relationship.

CLARITY, HOPE, AND RISK

The Four Buying Questions, combined with Tier Three Listening, give me real clarity on what potential Clients or Customers want and need. And that allows me to set aside my tedious 45-minute slide deck or verbal presentation and focus exclusively on meeting them where they are, not where I want them to be. "Cindy, I heard you say that the reason you started your business was to gain freedom from the administrative things you always had to do working for someone else. Can I share with you how I think our product/service could play a part in helping you fully realize that dream?" You're genuinely connecting what you have to offer to what Cindy wants and needs. Cindy's eyes are going to light up.

When we gain clarity on what our Customers or Clients want and need, it allows us to speak directly to how we can serve them. Seeing that possible solution, tied so directly to what they want and need, gives them hope, and hope allows them to take the risk to buy from you. In the final analysis, every business follows this process to succeed: Clarity about what you need gives you hope that our solution can get you that and the courage to take the risk to buy it from me.

Putting It All Together—The *Sell Less, Earn More* Power Triangle

Over quite a few years, I stumbled across and experimented my way to the Four Walking-In Commitments, the Four Buying Questions, and Tier Three Listening. Only years later did I have a BFO about them: These three together create the *Sell Less, Earn More* Power Triangle (see Figure 9.3 below). If you want to have a great first meeting with a potential Client, there is no better method I am aware of to achieve that. Life is an experiment, and I'm sure there is more to learn here. And yet for a couple of decades now I have walked into meetings with potential new Clients using these three tools in tandem. And I'll continue to do so until a better approach presents itself. Maybe I'll learn it from one of you.

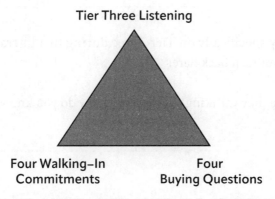

Tier Three Listening

Four Walking–In Commitments

Four Buying Questions

Figure 9.3: The *Sell Less, Earn More* Power Triangle

For 17 years now we have shared the SLEM Power Triangle with participants in our FasTrak business development course because we have found it to have one of the most profound, longest-lasting impacts in helping people land new Clients and grow their businesses. When you do these three things in tandem with one another, potential Customers will lean in and want to buy before you even have to sell.

My Next One Thing: Tier Three Listening

How will you use Tier Three Listening together with the Walking-In Commitments and the Four Buying Questions to flip the script from you trying to sell to them wanting to buy?

_____

_____

_____

When is your next appointment with anyone, even if it's not for sales? _____

Focus very specifically on Tier Three during that interaction, and report to yourself back here:

What were they thinking and feeling? How do you know?

_____

_____

As you listened intently and entered their world, what happened inside you? What feelings, sensations, or realizations did you have?

_____

_____

Was there anything you observed about the interaction that might have gone differently than you expected?

_____

_____

What is your Blinding Flash of the Obvious from this chapter, and how will you apply it?

_____

Who will you share your Next One Thing with? _____

_____ When? _____

Chapter 10

THE BEST BUSINESS DEVELOPMENT STRATEGY YOU'VE NEVER USED

*When I first learned the principle of Gold Veins, I was rebuilding
my business. I joined a Gold Vein, and within eight weeks I had
doubled my business—and in a few more weeks had tripled
it. And all I did was join the marketing association in my area
and asked the president how I could serve. I met someone at the
first lunch who needed my services, and my business took off.*

—Elvi Bjorg, owner of Elvi Bjorg Marketing

*Short-term thinking is the bane of our existence. Great
business development hinges on building long-term, stable
relationships that aren't focused on selling things.*

—Chuck Blakeman

See yourself in a room with 20 to 40 people, each of whom is either
a potential customer, a potential Lumberjack, or both. And then
imagine that you will see them all again, regularly, every week or
month, probably for years. And new people will always be joining.

How does it feel to find yourself in that scenario? And, knowing that you will regularly see them again, how should you approach them? Would you be hard selling to get them to meet with you? Probably not. The principle of Recency and Frequency would kick in here. You don't need to chase them or sell "at" them or stab them with your business card. Since you're going to see each other regularly going forward, it becomes more like meeting a new neighbor at a barbecue. You can relax, build a relationship, and see how you might "push each other forward." I use that inclusive phrase a lot.

Stop Networking—Build a Network

One of the built-in problems with networking we mentioned earlier in this book is that it can sometimes look like 75 vultures trying to find one dead cow. And the "dead cow," the successful business owner, doesn't go to those events anymore because they learned to *use networking to build a network* instead. Those are two vastly different things. Again, there is nothing wrong with networking. It's just a very helpful phase successful business owners and Independent Agents go through before we have built a network.

But networking *as a lifestyle* is a treadmill you never get off. Finding one customer at a time to transact with, digitally or three-dimensionally, is a never-ending hunting expedition. Contrast that with a very small "network" of Lumberjacks you will see regularly, who all have something in common, share the same Clients, and aren't threatened by the other people in the network. Instead, they all find great value in sending their Customers to do business with each other, because meeting their needs in that way makes them better and/or happier Customers.

As you build your business, you'll likely be Dual-Tracking: finding one-off Customers as you need them, but also seeing if they and others who will never buy from you would become

Lumberjacks for you—and you for them. As your small network of Lumberjacks finds its rhythm of referring to one another, the need for "networking" as a regular activity falls by the wayside. Finding Clients without networking looks very different. Instead of marching off to big event after big event to talk to strangers and stab them with your business card, building your business now looks more like what you would do with a neighbor or a golf partner.

What if we were 20 people who all had something in common and might see opportunities to push one another forward and connect on a transactional level, too? When we first connect as human beings on a relational level, we are much more likely to connect on the transactional level as well. Quite a few sales gurus have said these things over the decades, and they get applauded, and then they are misappropriated as meaning we should be friendlier, more charming, endearing, funnier, and nicer, but the focus remains on transactional selling to strangers.

Find Your Gold Vein

This isn't about working on your personal charm. It's about finding what we will call a Gold Vein,[11] a group of like-minded people who share something in common, meet regularly around that common connection, and are glad to have you join. All of them are either potential Customers, potential Lumberjacks, or, ideally, both.

It isn't about finding and joining a group because its members are all potentially great for your business. If you're just there to take advantage of the "easy pickings," it's no different from being one of the vultures on a wire at a networking event. People will smell you coming—we call it Commission Breath, and it's foul. Ulterior

---

11 Again, a thank you to Art Radtke for the term "Gold Vein" and some of the core concepts around it that we have built on for decades now.

motives are much more transparent than the "charmer" always thinks they are. "Authenticity" is a buzzword these days for a reason. We're pretty tired of being craftily, indirectly, subliminally, and charmingly hunted. Because it's still hunting, whatever adverb is being used, and we all smell it when it's happening to us. It's not what any of the gurus emeritus meant when they told us decades ago that people buy relationally.

A Gold Vein works to develop a Steady Stream of Potential Clients when you don't join it to get Customers. Instead, you join it because you love the cause the group represents and have a passion to be one of the people who is supporting that cause in the world around you. Rotary, a bicycle club, an animal rescue, a marketing club, the engineering society, a car club, a mastermind group, a church, a trade association, a members-only Facebook or LinkedIn group, a local sports association, a hiking club, social causes, nonprofits, writers' guilds, speakers associations—anything you can think to join that you would love to do anyway, even if you never got a single Customer. If it's not something you genuinely enjoy doing, it's not a Gold Vein. It's just fool's gold and a place to offend people with your Commission Breath.

The purpose of a Gold Vein is to help us create a Steady Stream of Potential Clients by serving, not selling or stabbing strangers with our business cards. A sculptor in my city has never had a business card, a brochure, or, outrageously, even a website. And yet she makes a very good living selling her art. The marketing world would tell her she can't do that. But she is in a couple of Gold Veins that have worked for her for years. Between the four or five Lumberjacks she has created in those Gold Veins, plus the other members, her current and past Clients, and her friends, she has more work than she can handle.

And this can work for any business, from welding to accounting to insurance to wealth management to real estate. The exceptions (and again, you probably aren't one), in some cases, might be some types of retail sales on the internet and some brick-and-mortar stores. And even they will be much better off with the owner deeply involved in a couple of Gold Veins.

Joining—or even better, creating—a Gold Vein is a great way to stop networking and build a network instead. A Gold Vein is one of the very best ways to create a relational network, and many people, including me, have seen how it transforms the way we do business development. It results in faster revenue growth than networking, more consistent revenue than hunting, and much greater stability during economic downturns.

During the "Great Recession" of 2007 to 2009, the worst recession since the Great Depression of the 1930s, I was sitting in a coffee shop listening to a housebuilder confirm project after project. He told me he had 23 home construction projects going at once, all over $900,000 retail. It caught my attention because in our city at that time there was so much existing inventory in that price range that it would take seven years to sell off the existing inventory, let alone new homes. He added that four of them were being built on speculation, something that sounded like financial suicide in such a desperate market.

But as we talked, it became clear why his business was thriving in a real estate economy that was down nearly 50 percent. He was part of a Gold Vein, a members-only real estate and contractors club that had been meeting for years, passing Clients back and forth and looking out for one another. The real estate sector didn't utterly collapse. It "just" went down 50 percent. Only half the houses were selling that usually sold, but that was still thousands of houses. So the market didn't disappear—it just turned its back on those who weren't well-connected relationally.

As investor Warren Buffett has said at various points throughout his career, "When the tide goes out, you learn who has been swimming naked." In the early 2000s, you could simply print a business card saying you were a contractor, and you would get all the business you wanted. You didn't have to connect with people or even be all that nice. Almost nobody in construction was paying attention to relationships at the time. It was a purely transactional market: "Here's my bid; here's your deck." Then the tide receded and the bottom fell out, and it became very clear who was swimming without a relational bathing suit. More than 50 percent of contractors went under during the economic crisis. And the guy I met, who had the very deep relational network, was brazenly building houses on spec and thriving. What a remarkable contrast.

Josh, an already successful realtor, took our FasTrak business development course in 2009. He challenged himself to double his income in 90 days, a seemingly crazy goal in the middle of the Great Recession. But he had invested in relationships and a Gold Vein, and when he learned how to intentionally and organically create Lumberjacks from those relationships, he began selling more houses every month than at any time prior in his long career.

I talked with one realtor at the time who told me she was leaving the profession, and when I asked why, she said, "Because nobody's buying houses." ("Well, not from you," I thought.) I asked her how many houses she needed to sell to have a good year, not just survive, and she said 24 would be great. "OK, do you know how many houses are predicted to sell in 2009 in the metro area?" I asked. She had no idea.

Josh knew that about 30,000 homes would sell in 2009 in and around his city, down from 50,000 the year before. To succeed, he only needed to sell 24 of those 30,000. He was selling an average of five per month because he had a Gold Vein full of Lumberjacks (yeah, we're mixing our metaphors, but it made him very successful). The overwhelming majority of realtors quit the market that year, which resulted in more houses to sell per active realtor than when the economy was booming. Most of the ones who left had been swimming without a relational bathing suit. A Gold Vein is a way to create a Steady Stream of Potential Clients that, along with the Drip System we'll introduce later, levels out the bumps and will get you off the sales treadmill. Gold Veins aren't just bathing suits—they are surfboards, too.

Buffett's bathing suit comment inspired me to create a simple line drawing to show why this happens every time customers get "scarce" (see Figure 10.1 below). In 2005 and 2006, the economy was "overflowing." You didn't need to build relationships. Finding work was like kicking the side of a bucket filled to the brim with water. This would set off some waves, and you could capture the business slopping over the sides. It came to you; you didn't have to go find it.

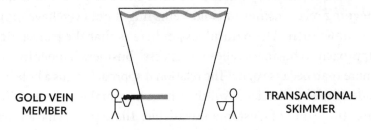

GOLD VEIN MEMBER   TRANSACTIONAL SKIMMER

Figure 10.1: The Recession Bucket

And then the recession hit, and like the figure above, the economy was no longer brimming over. From listening to the news and talking to small business owners, you would have thought the economy was completely dead, that it was 100 percent gone. I got in the habit of asking business owners, "What percentage do you think the economy is down?" I would get answers ranging from 25 percent to 50 percent down, or even more. Yet at its worst, the economy during the Great Recession was down 4.3 percent; it stayed at that level only for around six months. A full 95.7 percent of the economy was still thriving. Yes, real estate and construction were down closer to 50 percent, which is why I chose the above two stories—even in that space, people who had built relational Gold Veins were doing just fine.[12]

---

12 I am not dismissing the very real fact that a lot of businesses and business owners were deeply wounded during that time, and in many cases, the wound was not self-inflicted. But in general, the businesses most deeply affected did not have a strong relational Gold Vein network in place, and the ones that did well, did.

In 2008, the economy went down to 96.6 percent compared to the average over the previous few years. Figure 10.1 above shows that for those who had been living off the easy pickings of an overflowing market, everything changed overnight. At "only" 96.6 percent functional, no amount of banging on the side of the economy bucket was going to get any business to slop over the top. For those without good connections, it seemed as though the economy had truly died. But those who had invested the time and energy to build stable, ongoing relationships in Gold Veins might not even have noticed the downturn. The painful lesson here is that the transactional approach to business relies on "excess" business happening to us more than because of us. The relational approach drills a hole in the side of the bucket, so downturns have minimal to no effect. There are still plenty of Customers available. These people have learned the valuable lesson that mining stable, relational Gold Veins is much easier and exponentially more profitable than prospecting in the endless streams of networking.

Mining vs Prospecting

Eternally prospecting at networking events is hard, relentless work, while mining a Gold Vein, where everyone in the room is a possible customer and you'll see them all again regularly, can lead to a flywheel business that is happening for you, not because of you.

Most business owners are prospecting with a pan in an endless stream of networking strangers when they should be mining on property they already own with people they already know. We were all taught to sift networking sand to find the rare bits of gold among all the strangers, one random bit of gold at a time. Prospecting with a pan in a stream works, and so does networking. But let's take the long view on both prospecting for strangers and mining a Gold Vein. That might help motivate you to join (or start) a Gold Vein.

What is a prospector wearing? Usually overalls or jeans, usually tattered, and a dirty worn hat with a couple of holes in it from being shot at by other prospectors working the same stream. What is the mine owner wearing? Whatever nice clothing they want (see Figure 10.2 below).

	Prospector	Mine Owner
Week 1	+$150	–$5,000
Week 2	+500	–$25,000
Week 16	+36,750	–$375,000
Week 17	+39,250	+50k –325k (net)
Week 18	+41,750	+150k –175k (net)
Week 24	+56,750	+625k (net)
Year One	+125,750	+4,525,000
Process	Transactional	Relational

Figure 10.2: Prospector and Mine Owner

What is the prospector's transportation? A donkey or mule, or maybe an old horse if they're lucky. The mine owner has a nice two-horse covered carriage, and somebody else to drive it for them.

Where does the prospector live? Usually in a tent, cave, or ramshackle cabin. Where does the mine owner live? In a big house on the hill with the best view in town (see Figure 10.3 below).

Focus on Finding Gold Veins

Blinded by the Quick Result	**Building a Repeatable System**
PROSPECTOR	**MINE OWNER**
Pan for Gold, Find Some	Dig for Gold Veins — Rich Deposits
Celebrate	Hit a Gold Vein
Where Did Gold Come From?	Where Did Gold Come From?
Pan for More Gold	Stick w/ that Gold Vein — Mine It!
Celebrate	Build Those Relationships
Pan	Have an Exploratory Group/Vein
Celebrate...	Find More Gold, Faster, Easier
INDIVIDUALS	**GROUPS (That Meet)**

Figure 10.3: Prospecting vs Mining

What is the prospector doing all day? He's bent over the pan working the stream from dawn to dusk. The mine owner is taking their kids to school in a nice carriage and developing strategies for where somebody else will dig the next mine for them.

You get the picture. We can either find one customer at a time amongst all the other networking people who aren't a fit, or we can tap into a gold vein of relationships where everybody is either an end customer, a Lumberjack, or both. One of my joyful objectives in business is to answer the question, "How do I make more money in less time?" Gold Veins provide one of the best opportunities to get off the networking treadmill and have sales come find me instead of me finding the sale.[13]

---

13   We have virtual and 3D 3to5Clubs around the world focused on helping business owners make *more* money in *less* time to find Freedom *in* their businesses, not *from* them. They also function as great Gold Veins for the members. See 3to5Club.com for more information.

Why Are We Addicted to Networking?

For one, most well-intentioned gurus emeritus have taught us it is a mandatory lifestyle, when in fact it should be a stage that every business goes through and graduates from. It's a stepping-stone, not a patio. In networking, we're taught to chop down one tree at a time instead of just finding a Lumberjack who has already spent all that time in the relational Forest and can send us a Steady Stream of Potential Clients from their Outside Woodpile. Hunt one egg at a time, or befriend the Golden Goose. Chop, dry, and season one tree at a time, or find your Paul Bunyan. Your choice.

We may also feel like we get more immediate gratification from networking. It is possible, though not likely, to meet someone at a networking event and have them become a customer very quickly. We had one realtor go through our FasTrak business development course who was spending (not investing) 20 hours a week on average in networking groups and was making a good living doing it. The Facilitator challenged her to stop networking completely for the 10 weeks of FasTrak and instead, simply have coffee with people she already knew. She reluctantly tried it, and her business grew measurably. And she had a lot more time to invest in family, friends, and her life purpose.

Short-term decision making, a prime motivator for networking, is one of the biggest diseases in small business. We want that immediate cash result, which keeps us from investing in things like Gold Veins that might take longer to produce a much stabler, longer term result. We intuitively know that Recency and Frequency generally don't produce results overnight, so we get stuck on the treadmill of short-term decision making, always returning to the forest for just one more tree and needing to season another stranger relationship from scratch. We create a tiring business treadmill to run on forever, and we end up wondering why the business we were so excited to start has gradually become so passionless.

I encourage you to become "ambitiously lazy" instead. Work hard now at things that will bring long-term results and solve long-term problems. Focus on strategies that produce long-term results, and you won't have to work so hard later.

Build relationships; it takes more time and energy upfront, but a lot less energy once you have created your Steady Stream of Potential Clients.

The reality is that many people (not all) who network for years on end just to make ends meet are not the most successful in their field. If you stop networking and instead build a network of three to five Lumberjacks, Customers, and friends, and you use Gold Veins to do it, you are likely to get off the sales treadmill and join those who have Freedom *in* the business, not *from* it. It's why successful business owners don't go to networking events. They've built their own network instead, and they used Gold Veins to do it.

How Do I Know I've Got a Gold Vein?

Three simple tests let you know whether you're in a Gold Vein.

1. **Commonality.** Everyone in the Gold Vein has something in common that causes them to identify with each other. They're all engineers, soccer moms, animal lovers, hikers, realtors, etc. They identify as "us" because of that commonality.
2. **Density.** There are enough of them that getting deeply involved holds the promise of a Steady Stream of Potential Clients. You may be involved in some causes or clubs that you love, but they are very small or don't have any potential

Clients. That doesn't mean you should quit something you love. But you might want to expand to something else you are passionate about if you want to use membership in a group to help grow your business.

3. **Regular Communication/Gathering.** This is the key factor in whether you can call a group a Gold Vein. They must have a regular, common means of communication that you are allowed to join. Realtors have something in common and there are a lot of them (density), but they don't get together. However, the Realtor's Association could be a Gold Vein if you get on a committee or some other group that meets regularly. Without this regular communication, there is no Gold Vein.

   That doesn't mean they have to meet in person. It can be a social media group or teleconferencing group scattered worldwide, but they still need to meet regularly, and you need to be able to join them. We had one realtor decide she was going to join an engineering association because she geeked out on spans, triangles, and tensile strength. If she had to be an engineer to join, it wouldn't have worked as a Gold Vein. But they loved that she had a passion as a hobby for what they did for a living. And guess who they bought and sold their houses through for years to come? Simple. Brilliant.

What Is NOT a Gold Vein?

Analogies can be useful but also confusing. Realtors are not a Gold Vein, as we said above, because they fail the test of regularly meeting together. But a real estate *association* could be a great Gold Vein for a mortgage broker who can become a member and even a leader in the association. You can see two major things about Gold Veins from the list in Figure 10.4 below:

1. Gold Veins are *groups* of people, not individuals. Lumberjacks are not groups; they are individuals you'll find inside the Gold Vein.
2. A Gold Vein MUST meet on a regular basis, or you won't be able to build relationships well. A very active LinkedIn or Facebook group can be a Gold Vein, but remember: The closer you get to a hug, the more likely you are to sell something. It will take longer to develop digital relationships than three-dimensional ones, but it can be very effective.

Testing The Three Attributes of Gold Veins

Not a Gold Vein	A Gold Vein!
Realtors	Real Estate Association
Chamber of Commerce	Ch. of Commerce Sub-Committees
Estate Lawyers	Estate Law Association (Can you Join it?)
Divorced People	Self-Help Divorced Group
Builders / Contractors	Contractors Association
Small Business Owners	Small Biz Assoc's, 3to5 Club
Spiritual People	Churches, Synagogues, and Mosques
INDIVIDUALS	**GROUPS (that meet)**

Figure 10.4: Testing to Find a Gold Vein

How to Relate to a Gold Vein

First, let's discuss how NOT to relate to a Gold Vein. Don't come in selling and spreading your Commission Breath all over the place. Don't join for the purpose of gaining Clients—join because you love the group and want to serve. And don't join three or four Gold Veins; that's a sure sign you are networking and not really intending to get involved. With very few exceptions (no, not you), two Gold Veins is about the limit for anyone intending to serve and have an impact. I always think in terms of joining two and then once in a while kicking the tires on a third one to see if it might be a better fit for me.

Another "no" is to move on quickly to a new Gold Vein because nobody bought anything. Clearly you were there for the wrong reasons. And lastly, when you just go to the monthly lunch or meeting, show up a minute or two before it starts, and leave when it ends, it's going to be a long slog and probably an unsuccessful one. Relationships take cultivation and investment. It takes proactive time and energy to build relationships. Just showing up at the meetings and waiting for the world to come to you doesn't cut it.

Don't just become a member—become an *active* member. There is a world of difference between the two. You're there to build relationships of trust, and that will require that you get there early to talk to people and leave late. And you should be very intentional about getting "X" number of coffees as a result of each Gold Vein meeting you attend. Remember, you get what you intend, not what you hope for. If you just hope you'll meet some people, you probably won't. Intend to come out with five cups of coffee in the next couple of weeks, and you are likely to do so.

Along with being proactive, joining the leadership is the best way to benefit most from a Gold Vein. The more you serve, the more likely you are to end up with Clients who know, like, and trust you. They'll see you're not there to stab people with business cards, but to be a contributing member of the group.

Volunteering to be a guest greeter is a great way to start. Not only do you get to meet every guest who shows up, but you also get high visibility with each member who walks through the door. Being a greeter gives you the opportunity to quickly say, "Let's get coffee," and then email/text them later to schedule it. Even if a guest decides the group isn't for them, you might be just what they were looking for.

At the first meeting, it's a good practice to schedule coffee with the leader and ask them how you could serve. Elvi, our graphic designer quoted at the beginning of the chapter, did that with her business marketing association, and the leader asked if she would redesign their aging brochure. She was able to put her email and phone number in the corner on the back and got business from that. And then she met a copywriter whose business was rapidly growing and needed her to become his design person. Sometimes it doesn't take long at all to see the results from joining a Gold Vein.

By far the best contribution you can make early on is to simply bring guests and add to the membership. Almost nobody does that except for a few leaders. You will be instantly noticeable just by regularly bringing new people. And it's a great way for you to be recent and frequent with others. Just inviting them to the group gives you an opportunity to connect, even if they don't come. Once again, the more you serve, the more likely you are to sell.

Remember, Gold Veins are one of the very best but least used practices for building a Steady Stream of Potential Clients. Take the longer view, be ambitiously lazy, serve for a few months or a year, and you will begin to strike gold because you've had the patience to build relationships. Then you will be one very big step closer to getting off the sales treadmill.

My Next One Thing: Gold Veins

How will you use the tool of Gold Veins in your business? (Remember: Joining more than two Gold Veins can be too much or can communicate a lack of commitment. Stay focused.)

_____

What is your Blinding Flash of the Obvious from this chapter, and how will you apply it?

_____

Who will you share your Next One Thing with? _____

_____ When? _____

Chapter 11

FORGET THE GATEKEEPER— FIND YOUR GATE OPENER

I now get over one-third of my new business every year simply going fly-fishing, something I love doing. I simply started inviting others to do it with me.

—David Ruiz, wealth manager

There is somebody out there, not relationally far from you, who could rain Clients on you if you just got to meet them. Catalyst Events will get you that meeting.

—Chuck Blakeman

Let's talk about a proven way to make connections with people you would never be able to meet any other way. Or to meet that Paul Bunyan who would never return your call in the past and who will now be glad to meet you. It's all about one or two degrees of separation and the magic of knowing just one person who can crack the code with you through what we call Catalyst Events.

Catalyst: A substance that affects the rate of a reaction; (or) an agent that provokes or speeds significant change. Business Catalyst: Someone who speeds up the process of someone liking me and wanting to do business with me, even though that person has never met me.

Catalysts make things happen. They accelerate a reaction that might not even take place without them. Gandhi was a catalyst for change in India, significantly speeding up the process of becoming a free nation. On a micro level, enzymes secreted by bacteria aid and speed up digestion. Our personal lives are full of catalysts, and business has them, too.

Everyone can be a Catalyst for someone else. Psychologists call it transference. In its healthy state, transference occurs when person A redirects the good feelings person B has for them to person C. B is likely to feel trust and good feelings toward C even if they've never met. Because they like A and A likes C, their feeling for A is transferred to C.

For example, at a party, Don tells Maria he wants to introduce her to Ashley. They walk over, and Don says, "Ashley, I'd love for you to meet my good friend Maria. She has been really helpful in teaching me how to understand cash flow, and I remember you telling me that's a bit of a mystery to you. Maria, meet Ashley. She's my nutritionist—the one I was telling you made such a difference in my everyday health and might be someone you would want to meet. I'm guessing you two might enjoy getting a cup of coffee."

Maria and Ashley, two strangers with nothing in common, would now feel very comfortable meeting because of their mutual friend, Don the Catalyst. They end up getting a cup of coffee and decide to do business with each other during that meeting.

Think of the latent power in this. I woke up on one recent Tuesday, and an email was waiting for me from Don. Don, my good friend and business relationship, was introducing me to Maria, whom I've never met or even heard of. But I didn't hesitate—I jumped on it and scheduled a meeting with Maria right away. What are the chances of me responding if the email was from Maria? Pretty much zero. But because Don the Catalyst sent it and I trust his judgment, I'm actually looking forward to having coffee with someone I've never met and expecting something good to happen as a result. You can't buy that kind of catalyst power with any amount of money spent on marketing to strangers.

Let's take it a step further. What if you could meet six strangers at once who all like you before they meet you, and at that event, they all schedule a cup of coffee to have a Buying Conversation with you in the next 10 days? Would that be an efficient use of your time? Has that ever happened to you at a networking event with strangers? Do networking strangers tend to show up at your first meeting excited to see you with no reservations?

Catalyst Events are simple and small, and much more effective than giant networking events. Imagine holding a very small event where you only brought two to eight people, and in doing so, you meet six to 12 people for the first time who are already identified as very good potential Customers or Lumberjacks—possibly even both. And they all like you before they've met you.

And imagine trying for months to get past the "gatekeeper" for that one Paul Bunyan who could change your business, and that person shows up at your little gathering without ever having to talk to their gatekeeper, or to Paul, for that matter.

I believe Catalyst Events are one of the best ways to build a Steady Stream of Potential Customers because I can meet multiple people for the first time who already like me and are "warmed up" to do business with me before we've ever spoken. It's another cure for the common cold call because you only need to invite people you know, and through the invites of the other Catalyst (or two), you still meet new people with the advantage that they have a much warmer start to knowing you than if you contacted them yourself.

Why Have Catalyst Events?

As you might have guessed, the purpose of a Catalyst Event is to meet people who would never return your phone call or let you past their gatekeeper and who like you before they meet you. It is another way to expand your sphere of influence, get business by not pursuing business, be relational instead of transactional, and connect with potential Lumberjacks who seemed out of reach before.

How to Create a Good Catalyst Event

Our team and the people mentioned in the Foreword have done a lot of work on getting this right over the course of two decades. If you choose to adopt the concept but then start from scratch on the "How," I can't warranty your results. But if you follow these simple guidelines closely, you'll see why Catalyst Events should be an integral part of any business owner's quiver of arrows.

Small. Catalyst Events are very different from networking events. Part of the success of a networking event is measured by its size—the more people it has, the more successful it is. But how many people can you actually meet and have a nice introductory conversation with in two hours? If you're really skilled and thinking transactionally, you might be able to stab eight or 10 people with your business card. But if you're looking to build a little trust and get a cup of coffee with someone you relationally connect with, maybe six to eight tops, or even fewer. The other 90-plus people you sadly have to ignore or transactionally "get past" to find the very few matches.

In contrast, a good Catalyst Event is only large enough for you to meet and have a decent conversation with a few people in a couple of hours—maybe six to eight. I'd rather have four small Catalyst Events than one large networking event. I'll end up making four times as many good connections. Small events don't feed my ego as well, but they will feed my Steady Stream of Potential Clients much more effectively and with less effort. And that feeds my family, not my ego.

Who to Invite. Know whether the event is for potential or existing Customers, potential or existing Lumberjacks, or both. It can often be a mix of Customers and Lumberjacks; just be confident they will all want to attend whatever you are planning.

Two to Three Organizers. Catalyst Events also have at least two organizers, never one, and *never* more than three; that becomes a bogged-down committee. And we all know that a giraffe is a horse designed by committee. Everybody gets a little of what they want, and the result is ineffective.

Each of the two to three hosts will function as a Catalyst for the others. They will bring people you have never met, who are predisposed to like you because their friend has spoken highly of you. If there are three hosts, each of you can commit to bringing just three to four people each that you all have identified as good Customers or Lumberjacks for one another. In a two-hour Catalyst Event, you will meet six to eight new people who are great potential relationships for you and your business. And again, all of them will like you without having met you before.

Fun, Educational, or Public Events. Any event that your potential Customers would want to attend is a good Catalyst Event. It's *never* about the event—it's the cups of coffee that come later.

Some are educational and can be targeted to a specific profession, like engineers or contractors or therapists. Or they can be broadly appealing, presenting anything from a business topic to personal development to social issues. Some are designed to be fun, which could include anything your Customers might view in that light. Some are appreciation events, to recognize your existing or potential Customers or Lumberjacks for service to others, being a referral source to you, or any other kind of recognition.

We've seen just about everything work: wine tastings, indoor go-karting, golf short-game clinics, anything food related, crafts, hikes, game nights, and anything else you can imagine that might be fun to do with neighbors or friends. Some are public events you can take advantage of: concerts, sports, plays, movies, conferences, talks, comedy clubs, etc. Again, it's not about the event but the cups of coffee that follow.

Interactive/Relational. A good Catalyst Event will always have a strong element of relationship building, which means you should allow plenty of time to mingle. A movie or concert is not a Catalyst Event unless you do something like meet beforehand for dinner or afterward for drinks and discussion. A wealth manager and CPA I know rent a bus once a year to take Customers and one good friend each (who are likely good potential Customers) to a college football game. If it was just going to the game, it wouldn't work. But they have a 45-minute bus ride to the game, tailgating for an hour and a half, and the bus ride home. It's more like a neighborhood event, with high interaction and relationship building.

Exclusive. A lot of things make a Catalyst Event different from networking, and this is one of the bigger ones. You don't blast it all over social media or spam it to your entire database of connections. You get together with one or two other Catalysts, and each of you chooses a few connections who you would love to introduce to the others.

If each of you plans to bring five people, identify 10 or 15 to personally invite one at a time, and once you have commitments for five (or maybe six—someone could drop out), you stop inviting. The invite might look something like, "Sharon and I are hosting a [fill-in-the-blank] event. We want to keep it small and personal so you can meet a few other people who might be good for your business. So the other two organizers and I are only able to invite five people each, _and I thought of you_. If it would fit for you to attend, I would love to include you. Do the date and time work for you?"

After they say yes, right then or the next day (depending on your relationship), you reinforce the need to get a firm yes, because you have others you would want to invite if they can't make it. This is unlike any networking invitation, which I could easily give a very squishy "Yes" to and feel completely fine backing out of even minutes before the event. Nobody is going to miss me, it's a big crowd, etc.

Well-Planned. The two or three people functioning as Catalysts for one another will want to get together (virtual or in person) at least once to discuss the type of event, division of labor before and during the event, location, date, and most important who to invite for each other. Each of you should bring a list of people you think might be a good fit for the others. Then you can swap lists and choose the people you would like the others to invite, and they can do the same. This ensures not only that you can meet four to 10 new people but also that they are great potential Customers who already like me. Think of the energy it would take to get that many strangers to the same point of trust and goodwill.

No Sales. This is another unique aspect of Catalyst Events—there must be *absolutely no* selling, stabbing with business cards, or self-promotion by anyone at any time during the event. And especially not the 10-minute "how great we are" talk at the end of the rubber-chicken dinner, which was a bad idea when it was invented, and is a worse idea in the era of invasive "push" marketing.

I've heard many times after a Catalyst Event, "This event was different, but I can't put my finger on it." They were intuitively recognizing that they weren't being "targeted" in any way. You wouldn't target your neighbors at a barbecue, and you shouldn't do it to businesspeople, either. Human relationship rules don't change based on the setting. Treat people like they all live in your neighborhood, and you'll be better liked and sign more Customers.

However, that doesn't mean you can't blow somebody else's horn (just not your own) for a few seconds. If one of the organizers is presenting, the other organizer can introduce them, tell quickly why they have confidence in them, and suggest that everyone would benefit by getting a cup of coffee with them. But the presenter would talk as an expert in a specific field, not about their business.

At our Business Leader's Insight Lunches, which I held every Tuesday for nearly 10 years, first-time attendees would regularly come up to me afterward and ask what I did for a living. I never talked about my business during the lunches and didn't even have my business name on the invites or in the name of the event. When you serve, you don't sell. And when you do that, you very quickly gain other people's confidence and flip the script from you selling to them wanting to buy.

The only intentional business-adjacent activity at a Catalyst Event should be that when you're being introduced to one of the invitees, your cohost should suggest the two of you get coffee. Then you can offer to connect with them the following day to set that up. Otherwise, just enjoy the event and leave your new friends with the understanding you will follow up with them to connect on business-y things later.

One on Ones in the Next Two Weeks. Again, this is the *only* way to measure the success of a Catalyst Event. It is never about the event itself, which is only a vehicle for you and others to help speed up, or "catalyze," the transference of relationships. If you have a smashing event but don't make any appointments in the next two weeks, it was an utter failure. If the event was only "nice" but you got eight follow-up appointments, it was a smashing success. Be pinpoint focused on this result—it's the only one that matters toward building a Steady Stream of Potential Clients.

One-off or Regularly Scheduled. You can do one Catalyst Event a year or one every week, depending on what works for you and your Customers. A local insurance agent and CPA I know made a commitment to golf together every Tuesday afternoon from May to October with just one rule: They each had to bring someone who would be a good potential customer for the other, or they didn't golf. They would ride with their friend for nine holes and then switch for the back nine, and then usually get a drink afterward. That's a great weekly Catalyst Event. The bigger once-a-year sports event or holiday parties are also great. As with everything in life, build Catalyst Events around what energizes you.

A different insurance agent hosted a monthly lunch at a restaurant, rotating experts through as the speaker and co-Catalyst. It was always small—eight to 10 people around one large table in a private room. The speaker was asked to bring four people and the insurance agent brought four. So each of them met four new people who would be good for their business each month. You can see it just depends on what works for you personally.

Inexpensive to Profitable. Catalyst Events should never cost you much, and sometimes you even make money on them. One business owner created a Catalyst Event around his passion for fly-fishing. He recruited the Land Rover dealer and the Orvis dealer as cohosts. They got four great test vehicles and fully outfitted participants for no cost. A high-end box lunch provider handled food for them at cost, and a fly-fishing instructor did a half-day clinic in the stream for half his normal fee. They all knew the participants and the cohosts were great potential Clients and recognized this was a much better investment than chasing strangers through social media, radio, TV, or billboards.

As you can see in Figure 11.1 below, Catalyst Events are much more like a neighborhood barbecue than a networking event. They are uniquely relational, nonselling events that promote trust and confidence in each other.

Catalyst Event	Networking Event
Small, intimate, relational	Big(ger), showy, transactional
Serve, don't sell	Serve in order to sell
2-3 hosts	One or many hosts
Exclusive event	Fog-a-mirror event (for anyone)
Inexpensive	Can be very expensive
Meet 4-12 who already like you	Try to get 3-4 strangers to like me
4-12 Buying Conversations after	Get coffee w/suspicious strangers
Relational	**Transactional**

Figure 11.1: Catalyst Events vs Networking Event

Whatever Works—The Sky's the Limit

I'm regularly surprised by Catalyst Events I thought would never work that were incredibly effective. One savvy business owner got the local indoor go-karting track to give them full use of the track for 90 minutes at cost during the slowest time of their week: Tuesdays, 10:30 a.m. to 11:30 a.m. Then he got a pizza shop in the same complex to provide lunch for 20 people at cost. He and his cohost put on a $100 event for a quarter of that cost, charged $30 per person, and made a slight profit.

The track owner met 20 business owners and Independent Agents, many of whom had kids and a number of whom were now going to plan team events there. The restaurant owner created great awareness and reached 20 families, the owner's staff, and their staff's families as well. She gave everyone a big discount for their first visit to the restaurant, which was *not* presented by her (no selling), but by one of the hosts, who told everyone how great her food was. And the two event hosts got to meet people who were great for both their businesses, many of whom asked to be told when the next go-karting event would happen, so they could bring business owner friends. It's always great when your invitees start to build your Steady Stream of Potential Clients for you.

I know a residential designer, a realtor, and a mortgage broker who used finished renovation projects as Catalyst Events. They would give the homeowner a small discount on their services in exchange for holding an invitation-only open house for exclusive Customers to see the great design work and other features of the home. They put on a barbecue, and the homeowner was encouraged to invite their neighbors to show off the project to them. They were all potential Customers as well.

A landscape designer, a deck builder, and a window reseller, all of whom loved golf, got a local golf academy to hold a 90-minute short-game training session for half their normal rate for 24 business owners (three groups of eight, putting, sand, and chip/pitch), with drinks afterward in the clubhouse. The three instructors were encouraged to invite two people each, and the hosts would pay for them. The hosts invited four to five people each, and everybody either got new business or expanded their stream of potential Clients, all with people who were predisposed to like the hosts and the instructors before they even met them.

I was invited once to do an educational event for three friends who were Clients in the construction industry. They wanted me to talk about how to be Lumberjacks for each other in construction. One of the hosts got a great meeting room at their private golf course for nothing, and we all chipped in $35 to buy some very simple snacks. People bought their own drinks. And after talking about how to serve; not sell, and how to become Lumberjacks for each other, the 20 or so business owners at the event lingered and set up a lot of coffees with each other. And of course, the hosts filled their appointment schedules as well, with a newfound understanding of how to be relational. And all for almost no cost.

I've done goofy amateur wine tastings very successfully. With a cohost, you can invite six or eight people and ask them to bring one other person (spouse, friend) with whom they would love to taste wine. The rule is each couple or individual has to bring a bottle of wine of any variety that suits them, and it can't cost more than $15 before tax. We'll provide some suitable snacks, but if you have one you're especially attached to, bring it. No obligation. We put all the wines in brown paper wrappers and just write red, white, rosé, etc. on the paper, with a number. We then spend the evening mingling, tasting wines, and writing our completely uninformed opinions for each wine, on a scale of 1-5. These get tallied at the end of the evening, and the person who brought the wine that got the highest score gets a not-so-great door prize. My favorite was a Homer Simpson bottle opener that says, "Mmm . . . beeeerrr . . ." in Homer's voice as you open a bottle.

Get the picture? The sky really is the limit. Remember, it's not about what kind of event you have, but how many appointments you make after it's over. You get to decide what events work for you and your potential Customers and/or Lumberjacks, how often you do them, who you choose as your co-Catalysts, and how many people you think is the sweet spot. I love Catalyst Events because they are so specifically tailored to what you find interesting, enjoyable, and helpful, and what your Clients or Customers will respond to. Again, do what energizes you, not what works for me or the next person.

However, as I mentioned earlier, it's important to follow the proven process for Catalyst Events. A quick-start guide is below, but go to 3to5Club.com/SLEM to get the full "how-to" on Catalyst Events.

1. Choose a co-Catalyst or two, tops. Remember—no giraffe-producing committees.
2. Meet six-plus weeks out to decide on date, type of event, details, etc., and who each cohost should invite for the others.
   a. Date: Never one or two weeks out, and never more than four. Most business owners are living by the Tyranny of

the Urgent, which fills their schedules for the next one to two weeks, and leaves them with no urgency to respond to distant dates.[14]

   b. Event type: Whatever will make the *right* people want to show up.

   c. Invite the speaker (if any): Confirm a venue and get support lined up (lunch, go-karts, etc.). Planning six-plus weeks out makes more speakers and venues available.

   d. List of Invitees: Have a list of potential invitees two to three times bigger than you want to attend. Invite until you fill all spots.

3. First invitation—three to four weeks out, "And I thought of you." Communicate exclusivity.

4. Second invitation—a week or less after first—"I can only invite a few and need to confirm or invite another."

   a. Ten to 20 percent might fall out here at the second invitation when they understand this isn't a loose networking event "commitment", and that you are actually expecting depending on them. There might be less fallout depending on your relationship. Backfill with someone else, "…and I thought of you."

5. Third invitation—a week or ten days after the first. Share some quick news about the event, and "let me know if you can't make it."

   a. Anybody back out? Backfill, "…and I thought of you."

6. Fourth invitation—five days before the event. More quick news about it, and "let me know if you can't make it."

7. Twenty-four-hour reminder—bring X, exciting tidbit about the event, and "see you there."

---

14 There's always an exception. Against the FasTrak facilitator's advice, a financial planner put on a seminar with an expert on credit card debt with just four days' notice on January 5, a terrible time to do another "party". He got 45+ people to attend that very hot after-the-holidays topic.

a. Anybody back out at the last minute? Call people until you get the spot filled. Even if they can't make it, it's a great opportunity to connect with people (Recency and Frequency). I've invited people the day of and have found someone available, while making a bunch of great "Recency" connections in the process.

b. If you're relationships are not deep with the attendees (which is often the case), you could experience 10 to 20 percent not showing up at the event, even after your kind and regular communication. If these are people you don't know well, invite one more than you are aiming for, and if they all show up, great.

8. At event—no selling; build relationships and mention coffee later.

9. After event—schedule an appointment (a lot more later in the book on how to do this effectively).

10. Measure success by how many coffees/appointments you schedule, not any other metric.

As with every tool we are giving you to improve your business development, you can adapt Catalyst Events to your own personality and desires, from a four-person golf game to a couple dozen at parties or events. And you can do them as often or as seldom as you like. You can also team up with eight or 10 different co-Catalysts and hold one every quarter with one or two of them. The rules are very flexible, the intended result is utterly clear—create events that result in a steady stream of appointments the next couple weeks, with people you've never met, who like you before you say hello for the first time. It's one of the few, great, very underutilized ways to double your income.

For a list of 110+ potential Catalyst Event ideas, and more detailed steps on hosting Catalyst Events, visit www.3to5Club.com/SDS.

MY NEXT ONE THING
Catalyst Events—Getting Access to the Best Lumberjacks for You

How will you apply the tool of Catalyst Events to your business? (Note: some people will have them weekly, others monthly, others quarterly or annually. What approach gives you energy?)

_____

What is your Blinding Flash of the Obvious from this chapter, and how will you apply it?

_____

Who will you share your Next One Thing with? _____

_____ When? _____

Chapter 12

DOUBLE YOUR INCOME IN JUST ONE DAY (WITHOUT SELLING ANYTHING)

We raised our company prices across the board just 4.5 percent.
No Clients left, and as the owner, my take-home income went up 106
percent in just one day, even after leaving more profit in the business.

—THOMAS MAY, MAY LOGISTICS, INC.

Your market doesn't determine your price.
Your price determines your market.

—CHUCK BLAKEMAN

One of the easiest, fastest ways to double your income is to raise your pricing. We've seen so many business owners reach their income goal simply by charging a little more. And even if you don't think you control your pricing because the government or some giant corporation sets your reselling price, there is a lot you can do to overcome that. Keep reading. Pricing has a lot of head trash in it that keeps us from getting what we want. Let's learn how to get past that.

Freedom Money

What is the purpose or goal of pricing? The purpose is never *just* to sell something, but also to provide or increase profit. If the price only covers the expenses of the sale, you're in trouble. If it only provides enough profit to survive, you're an exhausted hostage to your business. But if pricing is doing its job, it creates Freedom in your business, not from it.

Freedom, in its broadest sense, is the ability to choose. When every expense of every kind has been taken care of, including taxes, and there is still money left over,[15] that is what accountants call net profit and what I more often refer to as Freedom Money. That's because it's the only money in your business that you can spend absolutely any way you want. You can take it home and buy a hot tub or leave it in the business and save it for the future. All the rest of the money in your business is spoken for. Freedom Money is yours to play with however you like. It's what selling is all about: Freedom Money to build a Life of Significance, to live out your Big Why. Nothing else.[16]

Doubling Your Personal Freedom Money

Let's forget doubling your income for a moment, which so many have done using these tools. What really matters is first increasing the

---

15   EBITDA stands for earnings before interest, taxes, depreciation, and amortization. That is a form of gross profit. The bigger your business gets, the more useful gross profit becomes, but with some exceptions (not you) it has very little use in a small business under $1 million in revenue. Our focus should be on net profit—the money left over after every single obligation is met, including taxes, depreciation, and amortization.

16   For me, business is about providing Freedom to live out my Big Why, and that starts with profit. If I don't have that, I can't have an impact on the world around me. And the more profit I make, the more I can live out the principle, "Give from your fruit, not from your root." For more on the Big Why, visit 3to5Club.com/SDS.

money available to improve your lifestyle. That's Freedom Money. Changing the world comes after you take care of your own root system. Your personal income has the same problem as your business income—most of it is spoken for as soon as you earn it. The money remaining after all personal expenses (including taxes) are paid is your personal Freedom Money. And that's our focus in this chapter.

What if you could increase your personal Freedom Money by 450 percent overnight? If your monthly personal Freedom Money number is $500 right now, and we could increase that to $2,250 overnight, that's an increase not only in your income, but also in your lifestyle, which is really where we use our money to create meaning and joy.[17] Remember, Freedom is the ability to choose, and when you have 450 percent more money to choose what to do with, it's going to radically change your lifestyle.

The Four Pricing Quadrants

There are Four Pricing Quadrants (shown in Figure 12.1 below) and they encompass everything from the lowest prices to the highest. The chart on the left shows the two Quadrants you should choose your Customers from: Low Maintenance-High Dollar and Low Maintenance-Low Dollar. Most internet businesses are based on this second Quadrant. For example, Google charges billions of people a couple of dollars a month. You can play in both or just one of these Low-Maintenance Quadrants.

The chart on the right shows the two Quadrants you don't want to play in. Nobody wants High Maintenance-Low Dollar Clients; that's an easy call. But High Maintenance-High Dollar Clients are addictive, and they can easily turn you from being a "Helper" to an

---

17   In my experience, I only have three resources: time, money, and energy. I need all three to build a Significant Life. 3to5Club.com/SDS

"Enabler" or a "Rescuer," and now we'll have to call you Florence Nightingale. I know from experience that the minute you drop a High Maintenance-High Dollar Client, you gain back the emotional energy to go find two Low Maintenance-High Dollar Clients who will help you fall back in love with what you do.

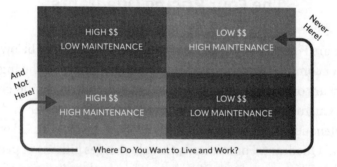

Figure 12.1: The Best Pricing Quadrants for Small Business

You Control Prices, Even When You Don't

What if you're an independent broker in an industry or profession with tight government- or corporate-imposed pricing constraints, so you can't raise your prices? You almost always can anyway. Start by moving to one of the two "Low Maintenance" Quadrants above.

If you're selling life insurance to individuals, it's a lot of work. A friend of mine focused instead on working with business owners to do a presentation to dozens, even hundreds of workers who would receive a discount that worked for my friend, because there was a lot less work involved. A mortgage broker or real estate agent with fixed commissions can move upmarket by focusing on higher-priced real estate that offers the same percentage of a much bigger revenue pie, but with the same or lower maintenance as lower priced housing. A realtor I knew in LA focused on selling Montana ranches to partygoers. He only had to sell one or two a year, and he had a lot of fun at parties. An insurance agent can have business owners as a preferred vendor to all their employees, or they can focus on commercial insurance with higher premiums. This same "upmarket" concept applies to wealth managers and any other profession with "fixed" pricing.

The bottom line: Don't be a victim of the idea that you can't raise your prices. Henry Ford was right, "Whether you think you can, or you think you can't, you're right." More on this in "How to Raise Your Prices," below.

Small Price Raise; Huge Impact

How does this work? In the scenario in Figure 12.2 below, we do it by raising your business prices by just 7 percent. The reason raising your prices has such a powerful pass-through effect—not just to your income but to your personal Freedom Money as well—is simply because, in most cases, every penny of a price increase goes right to the bottom line.

If you can raise your prices without your business or personal expenses also going up, the price increase generates pure net profit, aka Freedom Money. A small price increase has an exponential effect on your personal lifestyle—in this case, an increase from $500 a month of Freedom Money to $2,250. (And yes, later we'll get to your head trash around why you think your business is unique and you can't do this.)

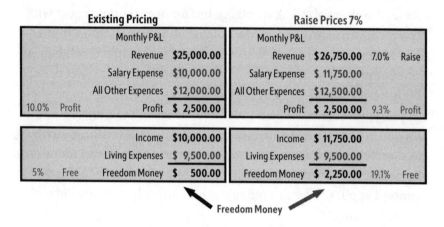

Figure 12.2: Price Raises Fall to the Bottom Line

Never Set Your Price to Attract Customers

What I really mean by this is that you should never think setting low prices or lowering your existing prices is the way to attract Customers. Never assume low prices will get you more Customers. In many if not most cases, it will get you fewer Customers. The following is an axiom on pricing that it took me decades to realize:

Your market doesn't determine your price.
Your price determines your market.

The least expensive production line car as I write this is the Nissan Versa for $16,390, and one of the most expensive is the Zenvo Aurora at $2.8 million (I'll take two, please, they're small). The question is, which one of these cars sells? The answer, of course, is both of them. The same goes for every car priced in between those two (see Figure 12.3 below). They all sell, with wildly differing prices from left to right.

YOUR PRICE DETERMINES YOUR MARKET

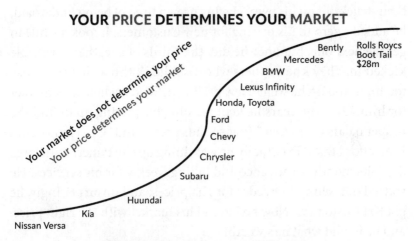

Figure 12.3: Your Price Determines Your Market

The reason is simple: Every price has a market. And wherever you set up shop on the Pricing Continuum is the market you will engage with. There are cars, restaurants, luggage, shoes, insurance, wealth management, and every other product or service you can think of for every market along the Continuum. And they didn't get there by comparison pricing or even cost-plus pricing (for different ways to determine your price, visit 3to5Club.com/SDS).

The price you set will have an enormous impact on your ability to reach a specific market on your Pricing Continuum. Most small business owners are under the mistaken impression they will make a ton of money because they are really good at what they do. That's wishful thinking. Nobody will start paying you more because you're great. There are great products and services in every profession and industry that are being underpriced and underappreciated by their Customers (and once again, you're not the exception—your price is definitely too low).

I know a website developer who started building sites in college for rock bands and startup nonprofits back in the 1990s for $600 or so. The question he heard most often was, "Can you do it for less?"[18] He worked for somebody else for a couple of years after college and then struck out on his own. Having grown tired of being underpaid, he added a zero to his pricing for new Customers. It took a while to get the next one, but once he did, the "birds of a feather" principle kicked in. They knew others who also didn't think that price was too high, and off he went. New pricing defined a whole new market for him. Over the years he kept pushing his pricing up to find the proper balance between "That sounds great," and "Oh, I'm not sure I can afford that." Eventually he was lining up Customers with large deposits months in advance and billing weekly for his services. He started out selling Mercedes for Kia prices, and unsurprisingly, he got Kia Customers. Now he's found his market with the right price, and he is paid what he's worth.

I met a talented but not famous public speaker a few years ago who nonetheless commanded the highest honorariums. He told me that when he first wanted to speak, he got the range of expected honorariums from a speakers bureau, and of course, newbies like him were not well-paid. He looked at the chart and declared his price was very near the top. The speakers bureau said he was nuts; nobody hires a newbie at that price. However, his rationale was not based on whether he was new, but on what he was worth. It took a while to get his first gig, but once he did, he was off to the races. Once again, the people who hired him also knew others who didn't balk at paying more to get the best. He didn't try to sell his Mercedes as a Kia and

---

18 Bottom-feeders are not always at the bottom of the Pricing Continuum. They can also be people who are always looking to get more expensive items for less.

work his way up. It was and is a Mercedes, and people should pay appropriately for it.

Notice the lack of head trash in his approach. And unlike the web developer, notice there was no elongated period of having to incrementally raise his prices over a number of years to get where he should have been in the first place. Don't be afraid to start at the price you eventually want to command.

I was once an advisor for a startup selling a "recovery patch." (Put one on your wrist before you fly or drink, and your jet lag or hangover will be greatly reduced.) I tried it, and it worked. I didn't care if the effect was a placebo—I'd pay a few bucks any time to trick my nervous system into thinking flying to Europe was a breeze.

Their cost per patch, including packaging and marketing, was around 35 cents each. Their initial pricing was far higher than I recommended—around $8.50 per patch—and they didn't sell well. They quickly reduced it to $6.50 or so, and the patches started to sell, but still not as well as they hoped. So they decided to stick two patches in the little box. Sales jumped, and off they went with an international rollout. The point? You can easily reduce your prices if you find they're too high, but it is sometimes a slog to raise them. But don't fall prey to that "slog" head trash, either—make your own business rules.

We're a Boutique

Ask the internet, "What is a boutique?" and the answers usually include attractional words like "sophisticated" and "fashionable" and almost always include the word "small." The website designer above became "boutique," the speaker started there, and the recovery patch got a very quick reality check and found their highest price possible with very little pain. In blind taste tests, Starbucks regularly loses to Dunkin' Donuts, but they can charge exponentially more because they are perceived as "cooler" and more boutique.

Small business owners suffer from uninformed jealousy—they think the bigger a business is, the more advantages and expertise it has. And they'll just never be able to compete at that level or at those prices. This head trash has crippled endless small business owners, from service to brick and mortar to internet.

Say it with me, "We're a boutique." Now say it with conviction, because with the rarest of exceptions (no, you're not it), you truly are a boutique! I gave a lunch talk once titled, "The Unfair Advantage of Small Business" and listed all the advantages you have over giant corporations and other seemingly threatening businesses in your path. You're local, you're in touch, you're incredibly flexible and can turn on a dime, you customize, you sell things the giants don't bother with, you are an actual human being who owns a small company, their "small customer" gets your personal attention, and on and on and on. It's just not a fair fight. Your advantages are truly amazing.

We can't get into it here (we do in a to-be-released book and course that are focused on what we call Hedgehog Marketing), but let this suffice for now: The worst thing you can do is price yourself 5 percent to 25 percent lower than the big guys, because you are competing against the only strength most of them have. "We're not personal, customized, or flexible, but we're cheap." Boutiques always charge more because they are boutique! Find out what makes you unassailable by the big dogs and share it with the world, at a higher price.

A buyer for a large chain of department stores once told me that he was able to buy a couple hundred discontinued lamps he usually sold easily for $350 for $10 each from a manufacturer. He put a $350 price tag on them with a line through it and priced them at $35 each, a very handsome markup from $10. After watching them sit in the stores for more than a week, he repriced them as $350 lamps on sale for $250, and they flew off the shelves. Sometimes a low price implies cheap, not thrifty. Be a boutique!

Pricing to Thrive, Not Survive

It seems obvious, then, that we should always price for profit, but small businesses rarely do. Instead, they look at what everyone else is doing and price accordingly (and, too often, below what everyone else is charging), without regard to whether that actually works for them. A great place to start is to ask, "Will this amount of profit per transaction provide the lifestyle I truly want when my business is fully up and running a couple of years from now?" If the answer is even "I'm not quite sure," raise your prices. If what you're charging right now won't provide the life you want later, it's the wrong price. Price to thrive, not survive.

Yes, I get that your head trash is telling you that you can't charge as much out of the gate as the "established" business down the road, but while that may be true in your head, it's almost never true in reality. And it's setting you up for all kinds of future problems because you deferred dealing with it now. After speaking to small business owners, Joel Spolsky, cofounder and CEO of Fog Creek Software, says many would come up and ask for one golden piece of advice, and he would just tell them, "Raise your prices." "But you don't even know my name, let alone what I sell," was a common response. That didn't matter. He knew that most small business owners don't charge what they should, so it was an easy lay-up.

Because it's harder to raise your prices later, you need to find out now if this business is going to provide what you want, not three years' worth of hard work later.

Fear-Based Pricing

"This 'raise your prices' strategy doesn't work in my industry/my profession." Well, it's possibly true in a dying industry, but even then there are ways around it. In one of my businesses, we did printing, along with direct mail, fulfillment of business collateral (paper), and a few other things. Printing was/is a dying industry already in the 1990s, and as such was and is a commodity. A commodity is a product or service that, whether true or not, is perceived to be of the same quality or value everywhere, so the only focus should be on how much it costs. It's all the same, so you can't charge more than the next guy. So we stopped selling printing by itself and only bundled it with our other services, and our margins on printing tripled. There's almost always a way.

So which market do you want to be in? Price for that one and thrive.

How Do We Know Our Price Is Too Low?

Most small business owners I talk to will tell me their price is too high, or that they just can't get more than they're getting now. All our Customers would desert us, we'd all be killed, etc. Yet almost every business owner I have persuaded to raise their prices did not die; actually, none of them did. And of the hundreds I've suggested this to over the decades, I'm aware of none who couldn't stick with *some* price increase, even if they had to back off a little, like the patch guys.

So how do you know you're one of the 99 percent of small business owners who need to raise their price? Two ways:

1. **Almost nobody pushes back on your prices.** When I share this in a group or at a conference, I can hear gasps and see blank stares of "instant recognition." Meaningful pushback is when a significant minority of the potential Customers you are courting regularly share a concern about the price being too high, AND a few of them actually don't buy because of it. Bingo. Your pricing is in the sweet spot. If you're getting regular, meaningful pushback and few just won't buy, good

for you. You're in the less than 1 percent of business owners with "right-pricing."

2. **Everybody pushes back.** That's right, almost without exception (no, still not you), when a business owner experiences constant pushback from everybody, like the web developer did early on, your price is probably too low, and worse, you are dealing with bottom-feeders. You need to move to a different market, and you can only do that by raising your price, because price determines your market.

Fear and Flo

Fear. "But if I abruptly change my pricing, I'll lose customers and starve." Then don't do it that way. The web developer continued to work with the bottom-feeders, but most new Customers got the new price. And as he gradually became established "upmarket," he raised the prices on all his existing Customers. To his surprise, a significant portion of them stayed. They knew all along they were getting a Mercedes at Kia prices. Keep what you have until you can build something better, but give yourself a timeline for making a clean break with your past. Otherwise, it becomes your present and will define your future.

Flo. I've heard a lot more objections to raising prices, but they all boil down to either head trash about your value or a Florence Nightingale mindset. Flo was a nurse in the Crimean War credited for working tirelessly for very little pay. With that mindset, she could have passed for a typical small business owner. Don't be Flo. Being underpaid is reserved for short-term, heroic situations. We want to give from our fruit, not from our root. Get paid well, develop a great root system, and you can serve a lot more people.

The Best Pricing Question Ever

There are three basic questions people will ask you about pricing. You only care about one of them.

1. **How much is it?** This is the worst pricing question ever. You need to sell value, not cost. Don't be afraid to say right upfront, "We're not the least expensive, we're just the best, and here's why." People who can't get past "How much is it?" know others like themselves—bottom-feeders. Be "boutique" and run the other direction.

2. **Are you my uncle?** This isn't a good question either. Sometimes you're the throwaway bid and you have no chance. They have an existing relationship with someone else and they're just going through the motions with you. Get out of these situations as fast as you can. Or become their uncle/best friend and be the only bid that matters.

3. **Can you do *that*?** This is the only pricing question you're looking for. When you help them understand you're doing something others can't or won't do, price is no longer part of the conversation. You can sell $1,000 laptops for $7,000 plus, like Apple did in the early 1990s. Be a boutique! Have people run to you because you can do things others can't, or you can do them in a way that others won't.

Be unique. Work hard to get people to ask, "Can you do *that*?" Sometimes the best pricing strategy is to make a great product or offer a great service people really want or others can't do. A new Client told me he had been called by a hospital to unlock their software systems, which had been frozen by a vengeful software director who had just been fired. They had paid a giant corporation $100,000 to handle it, and after 24 unsuccessful hours, one of them recommended "this kid," who was working on his own. He had it unlocked in three hours and charged them $300 per hour. I so wish he had been my Client at the time. Going forward, he raised his prices and charged based on what the market found reasonable, not "cost-plus."

How to Raise Your Prices

There are a lot of ways to do this and only a few that don't work.[19] Be intuitive and try the ones that work for you; you might just double your income or profit in one day.

- **Become the expert.** Become prominent, locally or in your industry, through blogging, podcasting, writing, speaking, or other means.
- **Become "boutique."** Offer things others don't. When you're unique and pay personalized attention to your Clients, you're worth more.
- **Fire high-maintenance Clients.** It doesn't matter whether they are high-dollar or low-dollar. It's one of those things everyone looks back on and says, "Why didn't I do that sooner?"
- **Move "upmarket."** For those who can't raise their prices, this is one way to make more money in the same amount of time. Focus on selling higher priced homes for the same work and the same percentage, but a much higher dollar figure. Or focus more on commercial insurance and less on individual, or on bigger commercial customers. Your price determines your market.
- **Focus on volume.** Again, this is a way to raise prices without raising them. Use your website, social media, podcasts, or an endorsement by a well-respected Lumberjack to move your products and services faster.

---

19   For the "Ten Most Common Pricing Mistakes" (correcting these could also double your income), get the PDF from www.3to5Club/SDS.

- **Bundling.** Earlier in the book I mentioned that we bundled printing, a very price-sensitive commodity, with our call center, order fulfillment, mailing, and other services and increased our prices and margins on printing exponentially that way.
- **Productize.** If you offer counseling, advisory, or other "let me show you how" services, turning them into products is a great way to make money while you sleep (books, courses, kits they can order). Another option is to increase volume by holding groups and classes, not just individual sessions.
- **Only raise prices for new customers.** Everyone else is grandfathered in and feels special.
- **Existing customers get three months at the former price.** A Pilates studio owner did this and reported that a lot of customers thanked them.
- **Stop doing free things.** Nobody expects that unless they are bottom-feeders. Enough said.
- **Change orders.** For everything from programming to construction, the contract should state clearly what the Client is getting for the stated price. Everything beyond that will incur a change order and an additional cost. The amount of money lost on "Well, I guess I can add that in" is staggering.
- **Funnel pricing.** If you have a number of products, figure out which ones can easily sell at a lower price and use those to create interest in your more expensive products or services. In some cases, we have offered some services well below market because they led people to want our core offerings. You can also think of this as "paid marketing." You can speak, write, or sell things below market cost as a way of getting your name out there and still make some money doing it. That beats paying for marketing every time.
- **Become more efficient.** Figure out how to do things faster without lowering quality. There are huge savings in not reinventing the wheel every time. "Process" is your friend

and a great way to increase profit without charging a dime more than you do now.

- **Deliver a great product consistently.** Contrary to popular advice, your greatest asset is not your people, your proprietary knowledge, or your market share. Your greatest asset is, and always will be, trust. And the number one way to build trust is consistency—say what you're going to do and then do what you said. People return to companies they know will provide the same great product or service every time.

- **Release your people to be great.** Too many small business owners are certain they have to make every decision. As a result, everyone else becomes a default child at work. You will solve so many problems if you learn how to delegate, and your profits will soar.

- **Require big(ger) down payments.** Don't start programming, building the chair, doing construction or advising a Client without money down. And ask for more upfront than you think you should. You can always negotiate. I never lost a Client by asking for 50 percent down.

- **Get paid at the beginning of each month.** If you have recurring Clients, never wait until after you have done your advisory session or delivered the programming milestone or finished the electrical installation in the walls. Don't ask; just put it in your proposal that you charge on the first day of the month for whatever is scheduled for that month. Clients who can't or won't do this will tell you so, and then you can negotiate. But always assume they can and will until you know otherwise.

- **10-day net.** Everybody should be given a maximum of 10-day net billing, including giant corporations, if you deal with them.

- **Late payment notices.** Get a VA or an inexpensive service that will immediately send a kind but direct notice the day payment is late and ongoing, firmer notices as the invoice ages. Remember: Don't be Florence Nightingale.

Raising your prices is one of the best, most efficient, easiest, and most powerful ways to double your income in just one day, not 90 days. Put your big boy/girl pants on, take on the mindset of a boutique, and do something for yourself for a change:

Raise your prices.

My Next One Thing: Raising Your Prices

How will you apply the tool of raising your prices to your business?

_____

What head trash do you have around pricing, and how will you push past that? What specific action will you take to do so, and by when?

_____

What is your Blinding Flash of the Obvious from this chapter, and how will you apply it?

_____

_____

Who will you share your Next One Thing with? _____

_____ When? _____

Chapter 13

DRIP YOUR WAY TO BETTER RELATIONSHIPS AND MORE SALES

We developed a really simple Drip System for staying in touch with existing Clients, past Clients, Lumberjacks, and potential Clients. It runs itself, and we can trace at least 30 percent of our business to that system. People love it when we connect with them because we're serving, not selling.

—BILL GRAY, BG LIGHTING LLC

Relationships don't need big splashes but a steady, reliable, welcome drip. They require that I connect recently and frequently. Business is all about relationships.

—CHUCK BLAKEMAN

Recency and Frequency, the two hallmarks of any healthy relationship, require intention, organization, and commitment. Relationships don't just happen. When our children were young, my wife and I scheduled a regular date night to intentionally spend time with each other as adults and get away from the kids so we would like them more when we got home (we always loved them, but we didn't always like them). We still connect intentionally with specific activities such as "Friday Night Lights," a special sit-down-in-the-dining-room dinner with Q&A, emoting, and empathy, and an hour on Monday mornings to talk about how we're feeling and what we're experiencing with each other, and maybe some reading together.

Most of you probably do similar things, including scheduling time with extended family and friends. We even make sure we take the dog for a walk with intentional Recency and Frequency (R&F). Yet in the business realm, it's somehow easy to just wing it at times and go with whatever happens to us instead of what we make happen. There seems to be enough forced interaction coming at us each day that we feel like we've done all the connecting we need to. And then we wonder why nobody is buying.

In the mid-1990s, during one of my two forays into working for another company, we had Novell, the software company, as a Client. I left that company in 1997 because of its toxic culture. After my transition, my main Novell contact was recruited away by Microsoft, which had become the largest company in the world that year. By Microsoft standards, he was a lower-level supervisor, which would get him omitted from most contact lists of companies trying to sell to Microsoft. But what most flashy high-end salespeople don't realize is that their best contacts in giant corporations are receptionists, admins, mail-room clerks (they know everybody), and lower-level supervisors, especially those who have just been hired and are motivated to prove themselves.

My R&F with him was simple. We sent out one newsletter and one press release every month, two weeks apart. It was nice if the press picked up the releases, but the main objective was to have another way to connect with our Clients and potential Clients. Getting a press release let them in on our news before the rest of the world found out. And everybody loves gossip. About once a quarter, I would call or email my Microsoft contact that I would be in the Seattle area to see potential Clients in the next couple of weeks— "Could we have lunch?" I never told him he was the central reason I spent a whole day flying from Denver and back; that pressure wasn't necessary.

This went on for almost two years, until one day I got a call from him saying he had just received my press release, and they had a project nobody wanted because it was too complicated and too urgent. "I'm glad I got that press release because I had forgotten all about you guys." (Seriously? I'd only been connecting with him slightly more than twice a month for nearly two years.) We took the project, and it grew to $200,000 a month in less than 90 days. And then we used that foothold as leverage to connect with other tech companies.

Let me ask you: Would you develop a Drip System of recent, frequent contacts like this to gain $2.5 million a year in business? Or, if you're a smaller business, $25,000 a year? If we're playing the long game, we all would.

But most business owners and Independent Agents won't engage in this kind of simple R&F, for the same reason they chase Customers one at a time instead of building relationships with potential Lumberjacks, joining a Gold Vein, or creating Catalyst Events. In our heads, we are all still hunting mastodons. That survival mode mentality promotes short-term decision making and doesn't give us the patience to commit to things that would rescue us from the endless drudgery of daily hunting forays. And so we live on the Roller Coaster Treadmill of Business, depending on reactionary sales. We *hope* good things will happen, but we never intentionally develop a Drip System to *make* sales happen. You get what you intend, not what you hope for, right?

Remember Donna, my sales director from Chapter 1? Even though I had $7 million a year in sales and all the other salespeople averaged $1 million a year, she still wanted me to stop relating with people I already knew via R&F, and start hunting people on the phone, one deeply uncomfortable stranger at a time. Building relationships rarely happens overnight, but when you commit, you can sometimes quickly break free of the circular pattern of always going back to the woods to chop down another unwilling, suspicious tree.

A Simple Drip System

When my friend Art Radtke would hear from small business owners about a business development activity they stopped doing even though it had worked, he would ask them why they stopped, listen patiently to the same pattern of excuses, and then say, "So what you're telling me is, 'It worked so well, I stopped doing it.'"

We've all tried some form of Recency and Frequency for a time. We might have even stuck with it long enough to have seen some success. But then life happened—or, more frequently, we just got bored with it and decided to have fun experimenting. One of the hallmarks of successful business owners and Independent Agents is that they don't get bored doing the things that work. Every iteration of the "thing" is treated like it was the first time, and our potential Customer feels special because they see the light in our eyes as we connect with them just as we've connected with a thousand others.

In some very real ways, I dislike sameness, order, scheduling, and predictability. I'm a wild-eyed entrepreneur.[20] I love being creative, spontaneous, intuitive, and opportunistic. So while I'm not naturally someone who loves "systems," I love what a Drip System can do for me, even more than I love spontaneity and novelty. Most people who do sales are like me, and all of us need to get onboard with a simple Drip System of Recency and Frequency that can generate its own flywheel and help create a Steady Stream of Potential Clients. The very attributes of flexibility, spontaneity, and intuition that help us in business development are also our Achilles' heel when it comes to staying diligent with a Drip System.

---

20 Entrepreneur is an advanced form of the disease known as Business Owner. Both are unemployable and want control over their destiny. But Business Owners have more sense and stick with the business they learned early on, continuing to improve it over the decades. Entrepreneurs repeatedly start ventures in areas where they have no personal knowledge, but they see a hole in the economy or an opportunity nobody else has grabbed yet (and they get in a lot more trouble as a result). Bill Gates was a Business Owner. Richard Branson is an Entrepreneur.

As always, I find simplicity to be the better road, and I apply that to developing a Drip System, too. It should be regular and true to its name, not grandiose or flashy. Noisy, complex rotor irrigation systems can lose more than half their water to evaporation and runoff. Traditional sales efforts, where we aggressively chase strangers (snail mail, text, email, calls, networking events, and online/offline advertising) are even less efficient. They're a rotor irrigation system on steroids. A drip system is 90 percent or more efficient. Less water. Less cosmic disturbance. Better results.

In today's crowded marketing world, we need a "less water, better results" system to break through. Having owned multiple marketing and marketing support services companies, I see marketing as nothing but noise. Some of it is good noise, some is irritating, and the worst is "white noise," the kind you don't even know is running in the background of the office complex, meant to camouflage other noise. Small businesses chasing strangers by call, text, email, etc., are almost all throwing their money down a rabbit hole of white noise. If you put $500 or even $1,500 a month into internet ads, you're going up against thousands of others in your space who are spending $50,000 or more every month, relentlessly. Your noise can't compete, and I guarantee that spending less money connecting with people you already know will be exponentially more effective and less costly.

The good news is that we don't have to stay stuck in a world of white noise competing for suspicious strangers. As I have already shown in this book, we can be much more effective talking to people we already know—specifically by being very intentional about developing three to five Lumberjack relationships. When we do that, marketing looks a bit like what we might do with our neighbors: sharing cups of coffee, golf, hiking, lunches, social events, and phone calls, texts, and emails with people we already know.

The Three-Tier Drip System

You can't be close friends with everybody, but you can stay connected with them all. A simple Three-Tier Drip System does the trick:

- **Tier Three.** A few monthly/quarterly/annual touches for everyone I know
- **Tier Two.** All of the above, but a few more R&F touches for 10 to 50 Tier Twos
- **Tier One.** The above, plus a few even more special touches for 5 to 15 Tier One existing/potential Clients and Lumberjacks

So who belongs in which tier? I have found the best way to design a Drip System is to answer the following questions in the following order:

1. **What is my "bandwidth" for business development activity?**
   In other words, what can I consistently see us doing as a company on a daily, weekly, monthly, quarterly, and/or annual basis for at least the next three years? If I can see myself doing "X" on a weekly basis for the next three years, it's probably a good start to Recency and Frequency.
   In this first step, ignore "who" and answer only "What?" and "How often?"
   a. What R&F activities already energize me (e.g., coffee, Gold Vein, podcasting/video podcasting, webinars, text, phone, email, Catalyst Events)?
   b. How many of these activities could I see myself doing weekly, monthly, quarterly, or annually without burning out or getting buried? Be honest with yourself. We regularly overestimate what we can do in a month and underestimate what we can do in a year. The hare in

Aesop's famous fable is all about big, flashy bursts of speed (followed by burnout and a nap) and the tortoise (who wins) just keeps plodding along relentlessly, one foot in front of the other. Herculean one-month efforts are not the road to success. Determined long-term plodding is.

In business, with almost no exceptions (no, you're not the exception), the tortoise always wins. What tortoise-type activities can you commit to in a Drip System that will change your business and, by extension, your life, over the next few years?

Example: "Weekly, I can see myself doing six relational calls, 10 relational texts/emails, three cups of coffee, and one blog post. Monthly, I can see myself doing two podcasts, one social media post, two Gold Vein meetings, and attending one of my Lumberjack's weekly happy hours. Quarterly, I can see myself doing one Catalyst Event (party, Lumberjack appreciation event, wine tasting, golf outing, etc.), an email/text newsletter, and one video podcast. Annually, I can see myself doing one big party. I can see myself keeping up with all these things for three years straight." (If you can't, go back and revise your bandwidth expectations.)

Once I establish my tolerance for "What?" and "How often?", I can start applying it to Tiers One, Two, and Three.

2. **Which Drip System activities will be for my Tier Three connections?**

Example: All three tiers will experience all of the following: an annual party, a quarterly video podcast, one of the monthly Catalyst Events per quarter, and my social media posts, podcasts, blog posts, and quarterly newsletter. As a result, my Tier Three connections will hear from me at least monthly and sometimes more without having to do anything specifically for Tier Three.

3. **Which activities will be for my Tier Two connections?**
   Example: All the Tier Three activities above, plus my quarterly wine tasting Catalyst Event, my Gold Vein meetings (if they are also part of that Gold Vein), two of my weekly relational calls, and one of my relational weekly cups of coffee

4. **Which activities will be for my Tier One connections?**
   Example: All the Tier Three and Tier Two activities, plus my remaining weekly relational calls and cups of coffee, my Lumberjack appreciation event, golf outings, happy hour, texts/emails, and birthday cards/emails/voice mails. Plus ad hoc attention (congrats on your daughter graduating from high school, sorry to hear about your accident, etc.).

Make Your System into a Process

As W. Edwards Deming, the father of process improvement, famously said, "Best efforts are not enough, you have to know what to do." As someone who dislikes sameness, order, scheduling, and predictability, I don't like processes, either. But I selectively love what they do for me and for our business. And I should, because Deming estimated that 94 percent of failure is caused by cracks in the system, not the individual's performance capabilities.[21]

The most successful salespeople almost all have a process they built over time (not a rote, canned "everyone-should-do-exactly-the-same-thing" process). Remember Sarah Golson from Chapter 3, who went from $150,000 a year to $290,000 a year in just 90 days? She told me she did it by trashing her complicated CRM and adopting the simple Lumberjack Buying System from Chapter 2. She gained Utter Clarity about two things:

---

21 *"Appreciation for a System" (deming.org/appreciation-for-a-system)*

1. Where each person was in the buying process (Outside Woodpile, Inside Woodpile, On the Fire)
2. The Next One Thing she needed to do to move them to the next stage

She was already a great salesperson, but she was exponentially more effective now that she had this simple, written process. (If it's not written, it's not a process.)

A Drip System is another way to help us double our personal income or business revenue. When we faithfully execute on simple processes, we do better in life and in business. My problem is I'm terrible at running processes. But there's always a way, depending on where you are in the business cycle.

If you have one or more people working for you and you've chosen well, you've hired someone who is your opposite to cover for your business challenges so you can focus on your strengths. If you dislike running processes and being held to the regularity that creates success, get someone else to run them for you so you can just "show up." If you are starting out or are on your own, you can find great people on any of the freelance job boards to help you run the process.

I would never do this Drip System stuff myself. It would hurt my brain, my heart, and my energy, and as a result, it would harm my ability to focus on the things I'm good at. One of our faithful "systems-focused" people, our Chief Results Officer Megan Kauffman (thanks, Megan), with the support of our Chief Dot Connector Mark Bellestri, builds simple maps to run our Drip System. We call these Freedom Maps[22]—they free everyone to focus on the highest and best use of their time and talents. Megan gets to her highest and best by running these processes, and I get to mine

---

22 Freedom Maps are a set of text boxes and arrows that can fit on one side of a piece of paper and tell the whole, simple linear story of the process with Utter Clarity.

by responding to her when things are heating up and she thinks a handoff is appropriate.

Figure 13.1 below shows a subprocess developed by Megan and Mark to help them establish Recency and Frequency in our social media presence. I'm purposely not showing you our overall Drip System Process Map because my system isn't yours, and it shouldn't be. You should have a unique approach that energizes you, using the elements of business development we have shared throughout this book. But I will tell you our overall map is even simpler than the following subprocess and includes calls/texts/emails, cups of coffee, podcasts, blogs, speaking, writing, Gold Veins, Catalyst Events, and a party or two. The following is just to encourage you to stop winging it. If the thought makes your heart sag, get somebody else to create your Drip System map.

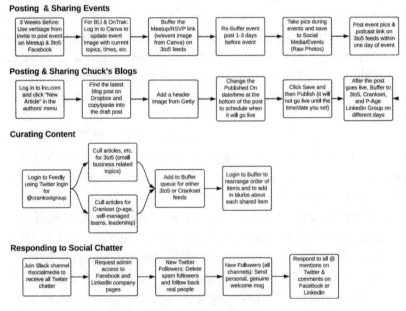

Figure 13.1: Social Media Drip Processes

A final reminder: A good Drip System is built around people actually wanting to hear from you because you are serving them in those connections, not "selling at" them. As a simple example, I get a monthly email from a realtor I always open because it doesn't talk about how great she is or what house she just sold—instead, it has useful information about the local real estate market, which I'm invested in.

In the 2010s, I did a lunch talk around this idea of getting people to respond to your Drip System. Together, we all decided on the salesperson we would least like to hear from: a used car salesperson (lawyer came in second). Then we invested 20 minutes thinking of things a used car salesperson could do to make us want to hear from them. It was amazing what we came up with together, like getting a birthday card, receiving an email that your high school football team is doing a car wash at the car dealership, a link to research on what your car is worth right now, an email showing the top five features or fixes that will make your car worth more or less when you sell it, and many more. None of which promoted the dealership itself in any way. Whatever you do to create Recency and Frequency, try things that will meet people where *they* are, not where *you* want them to be. If we want to *Sell Less, Earn More, then we s*erve; we don't sell.

Stop reinventing the wheel. Use your Drip System to create a Steady Stream of Potential Clients to feed your Three C's activity—Connections, (Buying) Conversations, and Customers.

And then . . . drip away.

My Next One Thing: Drip Systems

Building a Steady Stream of Potential Clients requires you to apply Recency and Frequency to these relationships. How recently and how frequently have you connected with them? How will you apply the practice of having a Drip System to your business? If you already have one, does it need revising? If you don't have one, when this week will you create one? Don't put it off. It's the most important "system" most businesses never create.

_____

What head trash do you have around having a simple weekly/quarterly/annual Drip System, and how will you push past that? What specific action will you take to do so, and by when?

_____

What is your Blinding Flash of the Obvious from this chapter, and how will you apply it?

_____

Who will you share your Next One Thing with? _____

_____ When? _____

Chapter 14

BAD PLANS ARE YOUR
BEST FRIEND

*I've been addicted to planning all my life. It was life-changing to
realize how to get moving without knowing every detail and develop a
plan as I'm moving. I applied it first to business development, but it's
a principle our whole company embraces in every department now.*

—Jenna Rodriguez, Applied Dynamics LLC

*It's not how good your plan is that matters, but how
committed you are to the result you want. Planning doesn't
create movement. Movement creates the plan.*

—Chuck Blakeman

I'm an eternal optimist. For the first five or six businesses I built,
I believed that the more careful planning I did, the better things
would go. Sometimes I'm a slow learner. It took me a couple of decades
to learn that there is an inviolate and immovable law of diminishing
returns to planning. And when it comes to business planning, the
return diminishes very early on in the planning process. Business
planning follows much the same path as heavyweight boxer Mike
Tyson found in preparing for a fight: "Everybody has a plan until
they get punched in the mouth." And as a result, highly detailed

planning is never helpful in business. Ever. It's necessary to put a human on the moon, yet only two business owners that I'm aware of are trying to do that. Stop treating your plan like a cosmic event.

Tyson is not alone in his discovery. In the late 1800s, Prussian military commander Helmuth von Moltke stated, "No battle plan survives its first encounter with the enemy." Apparently I'm not the only slow learner, because a few decades later a successor of von Moltke's, Alfred von Schlieffen, developed a plan to invade Europe at the beginning of World War I that was so detailed it included how to resupply shoelaces to the front lines. As his troops got hit in the mouth, it fell apart within the first few days. He forgot to ask the rest of the world how it would interact with his plan.

But we can't help ourselves. Research shows that the worst of human conditions is uncertainty. And again, I can't help adding, it's also the best, because it's where we are our most creative, innovative selves. But since we're still in survival mode and hunting mastodons in our head, we want a floodlight that shows us the path for the next few years. What we get is a penlight that usually reveals nothing more than the next step. Let the adventure begin.

No Such Thing as Good Plans

I want to disabuse you of the idea that there is such a thing as a good plan. Good plans only exist in theory and on paper. This is usually not because there wasn't good planning—it's because the world interacts with our plan in ways we could never have predicted as soon as we leave the office and get into the boxing ring of life. Management professor and author Jim Collins wrote a great book, *Good to Great*, in which he rightly demonstrated that *good* is often the enemy of *great*. But more often, I have experienced that *great* is in fact the enemy of *good enough*. A "minimal viable product" is enough to begin with. When Amazon was in infancy, Jeff Bezos packed books in boxes in his basement. It was good enough, and he got to great simply because he got moving on "good enough."

Great is the enemy of good enough.

It's not that we should stop planning entirely, but planning makes things worse if you do too much of it before you get going. Against all logic (but in line with intuition), most planning should happen *after* you're already moving on an idea. Plans become good because we've already gotten started on whatever we first understood. Moving on the plan allows us to interact and absorb information from the world around us, so we can react, flex, adjust, and end up with a much better plan than we could ever devise in the ivory tower of our office. The more we interact with the world around us and continue to adjust, the better the plan will get.

The reality is that good plans are only developed after moving on them. And *great* plans are only found in hindsight. Lewis and Clark, who were charged by the president to find the fabled, but nonexistent Northwest Passage (a way to get to the Pacific Ocean via water, without having to go the long way around South America). They only had maps for where they had already been, not where they were going. They knew a few critical things, like "go west until we taste salt water," and the rest of the blanks were filled in as they went. While their bad plan failed at their primary objective (there is no passage), it was one of the most successful exploratory ventures in American history. Most successful businesses also follow similar bad plans that lead them to success they hadn't planned on.

President Dwight D. Eisenhower said, "Plans are worthless, but planning is everything." Planning is the process of getting clarity on what you want, your *end goal*. Plans are what you use to get to that end goal, and this is where we get it wrong. We think we can create a plan from point A all the way to point Z and then follow it, as if we know how the world will react. We can never know that without getting our plan out into the world first.

How to Build a Great Business Development Plan

I said this earlier, and I'll say it here again, with emphasis.

Planning doesn't create movement.
Movement creates the plan.

The Greek mindset might have been expressed using the adage, "We think our way to a new way of acting." They assumed that if we just got enough information into our heads, our behavior would eventually change. But they were wrong. There's nothing anecdotally in life or in neuroscience or anywhere else that supports this. Both life and scientific research show us something quite to the contrary:

We do not think our way to a new way of acting. We act
our way to a new way of thinking, and even being.

No amount of reading about how to ride a bike or talking to people who have done it will teach you how. Get on the bike, get feedback from the bike, adjust, gain your balance, and keep going. And when you get off, you have been changed by the experience. You're a different human being, with a different view of the world than when you got on. And if the next person wants to learn what you have, they're going to need to get on the bike themselves.

There is only one way to get Utter Clarity on the Three C's and your First Domino. You have to get moving. Studying probabilities about closing ratios will not help you. Talking to someone else about their First Domino will only confuse you or even make you feel guilty you don't do things the same way. Comparing doesn't help. Only movement will create your business development plan. Get moving.

The Power of Movement

In my early 20s I was in the Army, and I ended up as the only ground pounder on the Marine Corps soccer team stationed nearby. They made me cut my hair "high and tight" so nobody would know. Our team motto was a mix of something General George S. Patton famously said ("A good plan violently executed now is better than a perfect plan next week"), which we morphed into our team motto:

Bad plans carried out violently23 many times yield good results. Do something.

We were one of the less skilled teams, but we made it to the tournament finals with that approach. Good plans exist in a vacuum or in the rearview mirror, never in front of us. Bad plans only get better after we get moving and the world teaches us how many of our assumptions were wrong.

Successful business owners and independent business development people do enough planning to figure out what they

---

23 In Latin, the word "violentus" has two roots: "vis" (meaning strength) and "-olentus" (meaning abounding in). In this motto, "violently," to me, means abounding in strength, or with deep conviction and commitment to movement.

want and then what they think might be the, first couple of steps they should take to make that happen. Then they get moving, and the rest of the plan is revealed as they move.

Albert Einstein was not a cognitive, he was an intuitive. Einstein praised intuition as a leap above mental acuity. He felt intuition was "a sacred gift" while the rational mind was "its faithful servant." The general view in physics is that he could not have come up with e=mc2 when he did in 1905. There simply wasn't enough information to lead him to even conceive of it logically, and he had no ability to prove it at the time. He simply intuited it. Physicists spent over a century attempting to prove the theory before they could say conclusively that he got it right. Intuition came first, and in 2011, 106 years later[24], cognition proved his intuition. It's no surprise then, that Einstein, Thomas Edison, and Steve Jobs all attributed their success to moving on intuition before actually understanding cognitively why they should.

As Einstein and Jobs show us, intuition is the sacred gift and cognition is the faithful servant of intuition. And that is how most successful business people approach making important decisions as well. In 2010, French researcher Frank La Pira published a paper titled "Entrepreneurial Intuition, an Empirical Approach," in which he studied 600 entrepreneurs to see if he could find anything they had in common that made them successful. He found that the number one indicator of success in an early stage business is speed of execution. The entrepreneurs would find something interesting, review it in broad strokes to see if it sounded like a good idea, and then get moving. And although they got started based largely on intuition, they continuously used the "faithful servant" of data and feedback (cognition) to make adjustments on the fly.

We're not as intuitive as we think we are. Our parents, the Industrial Age Factory System, the government, small business entities, and especially academia have all taught us what some

---

24 inverse.com/science/matter-from-light-physicists-create-matter-antimatter-by-colliding-just-photons

scientists refer to as the Precautionary Principle. The PP admonishes us to make a list of everything that could possibly go wrong and then come up with contingency plans for all of them before we move a muscle. Again, it's a great principle for putting humans on the moon, but it's a terrible way to try to grow a business (and, in my prejudiced opinion, not necessarily a great way to approach life). But if you look around, you will find most "experts" touting highly detailed preplanning, including nonsensical things called "annual business plans" as the key to success.

The Precautionary Principle fails businesses in multiple ways:

- **It rarely spots the real issues.** While building our list of all the "bad" things that could happen, we almost always miss one or more that actually will be the problem. You uncover the challenges as you go, not by listing possibilities.
- **It is unfairly discouraging and paralyzing.** No one is built to face 23 big challenges at once. I know multiple people who gave up on legitimate business ideas because they talked to someone at the SBA, or an MBA, or one of the other curmudgeonly other A's. All that cautionary "advice" made them walk away, and now they will spend the rest of their lives wondering "what might have been."
- **It gives you a false sense of security.** Webvan.com raised an enormous sum in the early 2000s with a very long prospectus detailing everything they needed and everything that might go wrong. They drove $4 billion right off the ends of the earth in less than five years—not because they didn't have a plan, but because they had a very detailed plan they followed slavishly.
- **It costs you too much time, money, and energy.** La Pira's research was pretty clear that people who get a germ of an idea and then move on it end up more successful a year later. They also have a lot more knowledge about what would (not could) go wrong than the people who applied the Precautionary Principle.

Resist the desire to Play Office. Resist coming up with a highly detailed business development plan to grow your business and then wasting time wandering around in a giant CRM database. Capture the few bits of data you actually need when you meet someone and focus on moving people through the Lumberjack Buying System— from the Outside Woodpile through the Inside Woodpile to On the Fire. Movement eats planning for lunch.

Chaos Is Not the Answer

Some minimal preplanning is essential, but most of it should happen *after* you get moving, not before. My friend Art Radtke, an avid sailor, inspired some great imagery around sailing to help us see how we've lost the intuitive approach that makes people succeed.

Question: *How do you steer a ship?*

Cognitive Answer: *With a steering wheel attached to a rudder* (Unhelpful)

Intuitive Answer: *Get it moving.* (The wheel and rudder are useless until then. And the faster you move, the less wheel and rudder [i.e., preplanning] you will need. While the boat is docked, you can throw the wheel fully left or right, and nothing will happen. But a little bit of rudder at 20 knots creates a very big shift. Planning becomes much easier *because* you are moving.)

Question: *How can you find the sandbars in a cove no one has sailed when you can't swim or fly over the water?*

Cognitive Answer: *Sit on the shore and study the wind, currents, tides, etc.* (Unhelpful)

Random Hope Strategy Answer: *Damn the sandbars—full speed ahead.* (Also unhelpful. You will find one sandbar—the one you shipwreck on.)

Intuitive Answer: *Get moving and immediately start taking sounds.* In other words, use intuition to get moving, and immediately start using data to see if what you intuited was right.

The cognitive or rational approach will leave you stuck in the sand. Random Hope will leave you stuck on a sandbar. Only the intuitive approach will let you safely sail out of the cove because it combines movement (intuition) with constant data collection (cognition).

Early on I used the cognitive approach, which usually left me on the outside looking in on good ideas other people had already moved on. I slowly learned that the cognitive approach ("perfect now, implement later") didn't work. Later never came. A few decades ago, I was taught the Random Hope approach ("implement now, perfect later"). It sounded right, but when I tried to implement it, it was just chaos in disguise and suffered from the same problem as the cognitive approach: later never comes. It took me a while to figure it out, but I finally got it right. It's a both/and solution: "Implement now, perfect as you go"—that's the intuitive approach. Move intuitively and immediately start working to get the data you need for your revenue or income objective.

Get moving, take soundings. In that order. The only sensible approach is to combine the intuitive (get moving) with the cognitive/rational (take soundings). It is the only way to be safe. You'll never run into a sandbar if you're regularly collecting and applying the data you receive while you're moving.

The Most Important Business Word You've Never Heard

Conation. It's a word I found in a book I always recommend to business development people, *Self-Made in America* by John

McCormack.[25] It's one of the most powerful words I've ever learned around how to "be" in the world around me, and specifically in business development.

Conation: The will to succeed that manifests itself in a single-minded pursuit of a goal. Or my slang definition: I want something so badly that I'm already doing it.

Neither definition fully captures the immense power and depth of this remarkable, life-changing word. Conation encapsulates "get moving, stay moving, never give up, and be relentless." After years of studying the word, conation is simply intuition in action. I get an idea, and my gut (or intuition) tells me it could be worth moving on. And when I do, I'm being conative.

THE SECOND MOST IMPORTANT BUSINESS WORD YOU'VE NEVER HEARD

Velleity. Quite a few years later, I was flipping through a book about the 1,000 most obscure words in the English language, and I thought I saw the word "conation" in the V's, which made no sense. It took a while to find it, but there it was, in the definition of another word, velleity.

I couldn't even pronounce it (vuh-lay-it-ee). The definition was what struck me. It started by making sure we knew it was the antonym to conation, and the rest of the definition showed me why:

---

25 This is the only motivational book I recommend. John was not a motivational speaker. He moved intuitively building hair salons in Texas malls in the 1970s, when everyone thought that was the worst possible idea. He conated through all the noise, and his book shares his success.

*Velleity: The true desire, with no
intention of doing anything.*

Conation moves. Velleity wishes. Our emotions can fool us into thinking we really, truly want something, like a Steady Stream of Potential Customers. But unless we move on that desire, conation is not present. We are just being velleitious (vuh-laysh-us)—just wishing and dreaming.

Remember the digital world of ones and zeros we entered with our First Domino in Chapter 4, in which one = yes and zero = no? When we choose one = yes, that is conation; when we choose zero = no, it is velleity. Velleity keeps us stuck Playing Office with "complicated" things. Conation, using the Utter Clarity of our First Domino, uses one = yes to get us moving on the few "simple" things that will *actually* make us successful.

Why do we get lost dreaming in velleity so often? My experience working with thousands of business owners is that we're just too comfortable, even if what we're doing isn't working all that well. I may not like the result I'm getting right now, but it could be worse, so I'll just keep going on the sad principle that:

*The pain I know is better than the
pain I have yet to experience.*

Velleity implies that I may not like the process I'm using or the result I'm getting, but I've learned to take two mental aspirin every day and just gut it out. If I change, things could get worse. But conative people respond very differently—as visionaries, not as dreamers. Dreamers talk. Visionaries walk. Again, get moving.

The Simple vs the Complicated

So why are you not "walking" at times? Often the easy "walking" things (like picking up the phone) are hard to *do*, and complicated things, like building a spreadsheet, are actually easy to do. Surgically removing an appendix is a very complicated procedure, but it can become easy for an experienced surgeon. The one who took out my daughter's appendix decades ago came and told us she was fine and then immediately boasted that it was his personal best time. It was still complicated, but for him it was no longer difficult.

In contrast, picking up the phone and calling someone is very simple, but our emotional and lizard brains can still make it appear very hard. Velleity thrives on the easy but complicated things that make us feel productive when we're really just Playing Office. Conation focuses on the few simple but hard things that will put us in Thriving Businesses camp (see Figure 14.1 below).

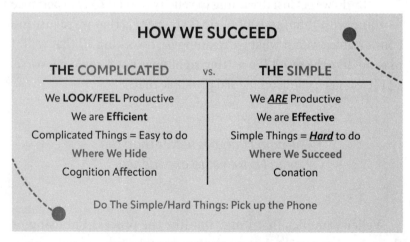

Figure 14.1: The Complicated vs The Simple

But we fool ourselves regularly with velleity because the complicated things are still impressive. Early on, when I was avoiding connecting with potential Customers, I would build spreadsheets about how great my business would be if I ever did anything. They were really quite impressive—I was even impressed with myself. I would go home and tell everybody how busy I was and how I did a lot of complicated things. But it wasn't until I stopped Hiding through Playing Office that I began to see any of the success I would get in my spreadsheet. Some lessons come slowly.

Where you Hide will be different from my Hiding Place. You might get sidetracked with any number of organizing projects, talking to people, attending events, researching products and services—you get the idea. Be honest with yourself. Learn where you Hide and put up a sign there that says, "Am I Hiding Right Now?" This will remind you that you should probably be doing something else to demonstrate to yourself that you are being conative.

The simple things that we *move* on are where we prove to ourselves what we really want. Do I want four cups of coffee this week? Desiring it is only velleity, zero = no. Making the appointments is conation, one = yes (maybe even a new Client). Be conative. Get moving and take soundings as you go. And intend to get what you want.

And don't fear failure—there isn't any. See your "mistakes" as seminars you learn from. If we shame ourselves for a mistake, we don't learn, and we go back to Hiding. So going forward, stop seeing them as mistakes. They're just seminars. And seminars have two rules:

1. Go to the least expensive, shortest seminars you can.
2. Try not to repeat seminars.

The Law of Intention

I've said this multiple times already: *You get what you intend, not what you hope for.* I call it the Law of Intention, and it asks a simple question: "Have I done everything I know to do to make this happen?"

If you can answer that with a yes, you're being intentional and you're in a great place. The world can interact with your plan and keep you from getting something for a while, but eventually, if you stay focused on receiving it, with rare exceptions, you can make it happen. You are much more likely to get what you want when you:

- know with Utter Clarity what you want (First Domino)
- are fully committed to receiving it
- relentlessly pursue it (conation)

Commit to the Law of Intention. Implement now. Perfect as you go. And, like the stream, be open and willing to change as the world interacts with your "going." Get moving. Stay moving.

My Next One Thing: Bad Plans

What is the one thing you can do right away to ensure you end up with a great plan later?

_____

_____

What are the three approaches you can take to execute a plan?

1. Cognitive Answer: _____

2. Random Hope Answer: _____

3. Intuitive Answer: _____

Which one works best for growing your business, and why?
Best approach: _____ Why? _____

_____

What is one thing you can do to adopt that approach for some aspect of business development right away?

_____

Where do you Hide in your business when you want to look productive but aren't doing the First Domino activities that will make you successful? (What are you pretending not to know?)

_____

What will you do to stop Hiding and get to the important First Domino activities you need?

_____

What is your Blinding Flash of the Obvious from this chapter, and how will you apply it?

_____

Who will you share your Next One Thing with? _____

_____ When? _____

Chapter 15

YOUR BAD PLAN STRATEGY: THE RUBBER MEETS THE ROAD

Any business plan won't survive its first encounter with reality.
The reality will always be different. It will never be the plan.

—Jeff Bezos

Bad plans carried out violently many times
yield good results. Do something.

—Chuck Blakeman

Now that we've thoroughly trashed most kinds of preplanning, let's reinstate a limited use of preplanning as a vital tool. Preplanning is very useful to:

- develop Utter Clarity about what you want when you're done—in other words, the End Goal
- create some metrics to measure progress along the way
- define a few simple activities you will find helpful for getting to that End Goal
- commit to the Next One Thing you will do this next week or two weeks

Salespeople Will Never Do This

Business owners and Independent Agents are, on average, more relational and less transactional, which makes filling out anything a challenge for them. They just want to go talk to people. I don't like filling anything out either. But I love what it does for me. Please remember Sarah Golson, who was a classic "don't make me fill anything out" business owner making $150,000 a year until she committed to using the Business Development Bad Plan that follows, and she jumped to $290,000 a year. By her own admission, it was simply because she used this tool, and she was amazed at what had been falling through the cracks. Written processes are more helpful than most business owners realize. As someone who gravitates away from "order," it took me decades to figure this out.

Winging it isn't a hallmark of talent, strength, or mental organization. We all need a plan before we start that helps us understand exactly where we want to end up, and it's always a good idea to ask ourselves what we think would be the best first step or two to get there—our Next One Thing. Then the plan needs to surrender to the adventure of actually hitting the Oregon Trail and interactively learning what the plan "is" or becomes in the moment, not what it "must be."

It's About the Result, Not the Process

Embrace the process, but don't get stuck on it. Other than a profound, conative, relentless commitment to your End Goal (doubling your income or whatever you arrive at), the process for getting to your goal must be filled with openness and flexibility to discover and rediscover principles, tools, methodologies, and practices that will get you what you want. Things that worked today may not work next week, let alone next year. Are you willing to commit deeply to the result without finding your security in the process you use to get there?

Always be reminded of and comforted by this:

The joy is not found in the destination but in the journey; not in the acquisition but in the pursuit.

Fall in love with the adventure of trying something new and different tomorrow to find the next Client. Hang on to what works and regularly replace what doesn't. Deeply commit to the destination, but also to the joy of the ever-evolving journey. As the saying goes, insanity is doing the same thing again and again while expecting a different result. Successful business development people do not practice insanity.

Your Business Development Plan (aka Your Bad Plan)

This is your most important document because it puts everything in one place to help you see and set your full intention. If you write it down all in one place and keep it short, it demonstrates how committed you are to getting what you want.

Your Business Development Bad Plan is different from a plan that runs your entire business. It is focused solely on the front end of all business cycles—your sales and marketing, or business development.

Business development is the first thing any business must do to get up and running; other than weak cash flow, it is the quickest way to shut a business down. It deserves its own, separate, very simple Bad Plan that gets better as you execute it. Remember, *when we capture everything, we do nothing.* Stop tinkering and get moving, and the plan will become great *because* you moved.

You can use anything you want to track your business development activity. I use the Business Development Bad Plan outlined below and recommend it highly. It keeps us from getting bogged down in recording somebody's dog's birthday in a giant CRM system that is largely designed for tracking long-term customers, not sales.

The Business Development Bad Plan I use contains the following elements. Figures 15.1 and 15.2 below show illustrations of my Bad Plan if you want to follow along here or download it at 3to5Club/SDS/Plan.

PAGE ONE OF THE BUSINESS DEVELOPMENT BAD PLAN

– Business Development Strengths and Challenges

The one to three business strengths[26] that energize you. For example, people, creativity, marketing, business development, operations, numbers, vision/strategic leadership, planning, mentoring, guiding, etc.

The one to two business challenges that wear you down. Unlike with personal challenges, don't work on your business challenges. Find others to do the things that wear you down and invest time getting better at your strengths.

– Who Do You Want to Meet?

Ideal Client Description. Describe your favorite Client, either one you already have, or one you would like to have: their

---

26 We developed the Apex Profile (apexprofile.com) to help business owners and Independent Agents identify their business strengths and challenges. Enter the code SDS100 below the $79.00 price to change it to $0.00 and have all your strategic leaders take it. It will show how each of you is valuable in very different ways and how you all need each other.

industry/profession, annual revenue, location, number of staff, slow/fast-growth company, department (sales, ops, accounting, etc.), gender, or other unique identifiers.

Lumberjack Description. This should be the same process as for your ideal Client. We would love every client to also become a Lumberjack for us as well. We should always offer to take the relationship to this level with them (and be their Lumberjack, too). But I have found that many of my best Lumberjacks never bought a thing from me, but simply saw the value in sending their clients to me and receiving clients in return from me.

– Your Lumberjack Buying System

Forest Process. Where do I find my ideal Client? My ideal Lumberjack/Paul Bunyan? How do I serve them?

Outside Woodpile Activities. What activities do I do to cultivate a Steady Stream of Potential Clients? Just list them here; you can describe them in more detail later (e.g., calls, texts, blogs, podcasts/video podcasts, Gold Veins, Catalyst Events, Instagram, LinkedIn groups, conference booths, etc.).

Inside Woodpile Process. What activities do I do to create Buying Conversations (coffees, calls, proposals, texts, emails, etc.)? Reminder: the closer you get to a hug . . .

On the Fire Process. What is my favorite question I ask to help someone make a decision? For example: "Would you like to give it a try?" (Go for a soft commitment like this first, and then follow with "I'll need your credit card" or "Here's the proposal for us to sign.") Memorize something and learn to live with a few seconds of silence. Practice on friends.

– Asking for a Referral

When and how we ask for a referral is important. Do we do it during the Buying Conversation, at the proposal signing, following up next week, or at some other time? A memorized ask, like "Do you know one other person who might benefit from the experience you're having/have had?" brings Utter Clarity to how you interact with people during a Buying Conversation.

Your Business Development Strategy Bad Plan

Try to fill in all sections without expanding the blue area—be concise and keep it simple or you won't use it!

Business Development Strengths and Challenges

The 1-3 business strengths that energize you, that you can use most effectively to build your sales

The 1-2 business challenges that wear you down, and how you will compensate for them (delegate if possible)

Who Do You Want to Meet?

Ideal Client Description—how do you know when you meet one?

Lumberjack Description—what industry/profession are they in? Who is the client they have that you want?

Your Lumberjack Buying System

Forest Activites Where I find my Ideal Clients and Lumberjacks, my planned activities to serve them

Outside Woodpile Activities Be specific—what meetings, connections will I do toward a Steady Stream of Pot. Clients?

Inside Woodpile Activities—What will I do to follow up on my Outside Woodpile to my First Domino goal weekly?

On the Fire Process—closing. (TIME KILLS DEALS)—what question or questions will I regularly ask to gain commitment?

Asking For A Referral

When? How?

Figure 15.1: Page 1—Your Business Development Strategy Bad Plan

PAGE TWO OF THE BUSINESS DEVELOPMENT BAD PLAN
– Your Business Development Triangle

Your Walking-In Commitments. Serve, talk when asked, intend to make money, and make an offer. Remember, you get what you intend. Review these walking in to every Buying Conversation.

The Four Buying Questions. Past? Future? Present? Ideal Client? Try to stick to this asking and serving process until you feel comfortable adding to or changing it.

Your Walking-In Commitments. Tier Three—What do others think and feel about themselves, and how can I enter (come alongside) that in supporting them?

– Gold Veins

Remember, be authentic. Only join the one or two you would get involved in even if you didn't use it to find clients? And don't just show up. Get involved, serve, become the leader.

– Catalyst Events

It's only a catalyst event with one to two other leaders. You get to decide on the frequency that works for you and how you're built.

– My "3Cs" Ratio Goals

The ratios of Connections to (Buying) Conversations and Conversations to Customers/Clients are critical for discovering your Leading and Lagging Indicators and for arriving at your First Domino (see Chapter 4).

– My First Domino

What is that ONE activity that regularly puts in motion the flywheel that creates every other activity in your business? It might be four cups of coffee a week, 20 texts, 10 phone conversations, one blog/video/podcast per week, etc.

– Summary—My Daily/Weekly/Monthly Strategy

This is a quick summary of the most important elements of your plan (cups of coffee, weekly calls/text/emails, podcasts/blogs, social media posts, and other highly regular activities). You should be able to share this summary with someone in one minute—it encapsulates the very few core activities that make your entire marketing and business development strategy work. If that strategy is too complicated to share by describing four to six simple core activities in three minutes or less, that's a sign you might be Playing Office. Remember, now that you have a First Domino, your world is digital, not analog. Every morning is a question of ones and zeros. You know exactly what to do; the only question is whether you will do it: one = yes and zero = no?

Your Business Development Triangle

Your Walking-In Commitments
Your Buying Questions
Tier Three Listening

Gold Veins

What one or two clubs, associations, or online groups are you commiting to? How do you intend to serve in each of them?

Catalyst Events

What weekly, monthly, quarterly, or annual events will you do with one to two other business owners to grow your Steady Stream of Potential Clients? How will you measure success?

My "3Cs" Ratio Goals

What is your intended (or known) ratio of 1) Connections to (Buying) Conversations, and 2) Buying Conversations to Clients?

My First Domino (The most important number I will ever know in business)

Reminder: It will either be # of Connections per week, or # of (Buying) Conversations each week.

Summary—My Daily/Weekly/Monthly Strategy (from above)

Summarize the above plan—you should be able to share it in three minutes or less.

Figure 15.2: Page 2—Your Business Development Strategy Bad Plan

Be the Best Version of You, Not Me

One of the failings of sales courses is that they are usually focused on getting everyone to follow the process that worked for the person who developed it. You're not a failure if you can't follow someone else's road to success. I'm a unique snowflake, and so are you. You are your own person, with your own strengths and challenges, and that will likely make it harder for you to follow someone else's plan.

The best salespeople don't follow rote systems rigidly. They apply broad principles and get very attached to whatever tools and methods work uniquely well for them. You will use the tools and activities in this book very differently from the next person. You might have three cups of coffee a week, and the next person will have 12 Zoom calls instead. You'll do a Catalyst Event twice a month, and the next person will do three a year. You'll focus on in-person contact, and the next person will do everything with a keyboard and a camera.

And you're both right—*IF* it works for you. Remember, success is quite predictable, *when* we do the right things. Get your Bad Plan in motion and experiment to find the things that work for you. Then be uniquely *you* and stick with whatever creates success for you; ignore others who are succeeding in a very different way.

It's likely there will be tools we presented here that you don't need. Find the tools and activities that are the most energizing and most effective for you and wield them relentlessly.

Sharing Your Bad Plan with a Support Partner

I strongly recommend having Support Partners in life and in business. A Support Partner, to me, is different from an accountability partner.

Maybe it's semantics, but to me, "accountability" conjures up sales managers chasing salespeople to report on activities the salesperson never wanted to do in the first place. If I'm holding someone accountable, it seems to imply that when I ask them, "How did your calls go?" I'm expecting that they didn't make their calls, and my job will be to motivate them and get them back on track. Accountability just feels a bit codependent to me.

But when I ask a Support Partner, "How did your calls go?", I'm already leaning in, excited to hear how the calls went, and I'd be surprised if they hadn't happened. A Support Partner doesn't exist to force me to succeed. They're a resource, a guide, some "outside eyes" on my processes, and yes, at times, someone to lean on for a bit of encouragement to get back on the horse. A Support Partner is glad to help motivate me at times; an accountability partner feels it is their *job* to motivate me.

I love support, but I shy away from accountability. Again, this all might feel like semantics to you, but having worked for a few sales managers early on, I have found that moving away from accountability and toward support has been very helpful in getting where I want to go in business.

And again, I beat this drum, gently and relentlessly: You get what you intend, not what you hope for. If you have a written plan, it shows intention. If you have a plan only in your head, it demonstrates an unwitting commitment to the Random Hope Strategy of Business. Be intentional. Write down what you want and chase it with everything you've got.

My Next One Thing: Your Written Business Development Plan

If you already have a written business development plan, congratulations. Does it need updating? If you don't have a written one, specifically when (day and time of day) will you have this completed? Stop reinventing the wheel and put your marketing and sales activities all on one form. Use ours or develop your own— whatever works best for you. Keep it simple and short—make it something you could share with someone in three minutes.

What is your Next One Thing around having a written business development plan? Remember, they are never perfect, but they will only get better if you start with an imperfect plan and get moving on it.

_____

What is your Blinding Flash of the Obvious from this chapter, and how will you apply it?

_____

Who will you share your Next One Thing with? _____

_____ When? _____

Chapter 16

GET WHAT YOU INTEND— BLOCK IT IN

*I don't like block scheduling at all. I just like
what it does for me. So I do it; sparingly.*

—CHUCK BLAKEMAN

*Block scheduling is the secret sauce to
achieving your goals and objectives.*

—MARK BELLESTRI, PROMISE CARE, INC.

Most people who love sales will want to skip this chapter. To many, block scheduling seems confining and rigid. As I have mentioned before, I shy away from sameness, order, scheduling, and predictability and lean toward being creative, spontaneous, intuitive, and opportunistic. So it's no surprise I'm not a "block scheduler."

I'm not asking you to become someone who schedules out every minute in your calendar. I'm asking you to consider being intentional about your Three C's:

- **Connections.** Make X calls to potential Customers and/or Lumberjacks.
- **Conversations (Buying).** Have X meetings (online or in person).

- **Clients/Customers.** Acquire a new one.

Then do whatever you can to turn that intention into reality. Remember, now that we have a First Domino, we have left the analog business world of infinite possibilities and moved to our digital world of ones and zeros. "Am I going to schedule those Conversations for next week, yes/no?" Don't Hide. Don't Play Office. And don't leave success up to chance by relying on the Random Hope Strategy of Business.

Figure 16.1 below shows a real weekly calendar from when I first started Crankset Group and began building 3to5 Clubs. You'll notice there are a lot of blanks in my schedule, for two reasons:

1. Block scheduling my whole week would give me claustrophobia. It took years and even decades to learn that I should honor and promote my business strengths and compensate for my weaknesses. So I didn't try to become a block scheduler. Instead, I just used it lightly to help me stay focused and intentional.

2. I didn't have existing customers when this was my schedule. My sole focus was on Client acquisition using the Lumberjack Buying System, a First Domino, the Four Commitments, the Four Buying Questions, Tier Three Thinking, a couple of Gold Veins, and a few scattered Catalyst Events. I scheduled only the very important activities that would help me execute on my First Domino and reach my goal of one new Client per week.

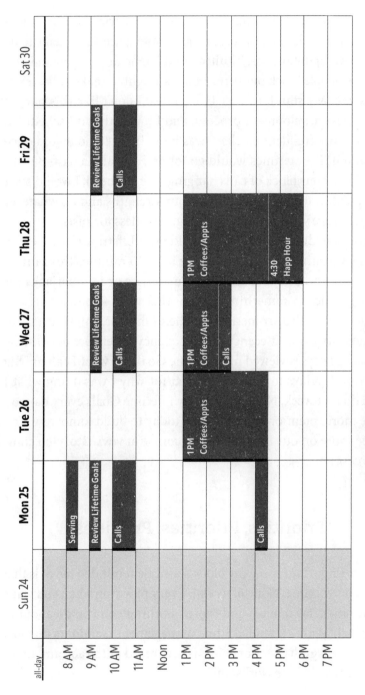

Figure 16.1: Block Scheduling—Freedom in Your Business

As I picked up Customers, they could be serviced in the spaces between the blocks, and the big areas of white space allowed me to be the creative, spontaneous, intuitive, and opportunistic person I am.

Some people block out three hours straight to make calls, texts, emails, etc. My standard was 45 minutes. I don't like this part of the business development process, and I found that if I scheduled smaller, more frequent blocks, I was more likely to do it, and once I got into it, I sometimes would go for an hour and a half. But if I had a three-hour block of calls hanging over my head, I would start Playing Office to avoid it. Go with your strengths and do whatever will encourage you to be the plodding, relentless tortoise.

I also scheduled "Serving" and "Review Lifetime Goals" every Monday morning. The Serving time is 10-15 minutes thinking of one to three potential or existing Customers or Lumberjacks for whom I could do something helpful that week—send an article, make a referral, drop something by their office, or simply text them an appreciative note. Recency and Frequency never goes out of style.

And I always reviewed my Lifetime Goals, or what I call my Big Why, on Mondays to give me context for why I was doing what I would do that week. Now I review my Lifetime Goals every day so I can be more intentional about using today to build tomorrow. You can see more on our Lifetime Goals course at www.3to5club.com/resources/.

Priorities, Priorities, Priorities

Another important thing my block schedule reminded me of is that I can't control time. None of us can. Every morning when you wake up, the clock has moved, and there's nothing you can do about it. In my early years I attended "time management" seminars that just made me feel guilty for not being as organized as the accountant or engineer who led the workshop.

Other gurus tried to shift the focus from managing time to managing actions. This hit closer for me, but it still begs the question, "Which actions are most important?" In the past 20 years or so, I have changed my focus from time management to managing *priorities*. My mother justifiably cornered me once with the following statement on homework:

> *Chuck, there's no such thing as excuses, there's not even reasons. There are only priorities.*

I had to grudgingly admit she was right. We *always*, 100 percent of the time, do what's most important. Everyone's top four priorities in life are breathing, eating, sleeping, and going to the bathroom. How do we know this? Because we must do them regularly to survive. Priorities don't live in a dream world. They move from our heads, through our hearts, into our bodies, and spring forth from our hands. Priority management is the most important personal discipline you can have in business: Figure out who/what is most important, put it at the top of your list, and don't move on to the next "action" until it's done, no matter how much time the priority takes.

What is your top priority? If building your business is important, acquiring customers is at the top of the list of things that will make that happen. That makes your First Domino, your Connections, and your (Buying) Conversations the most important priorities you have as you grow. And if you want to be free from the Roller Coaster Treadmill of Business we talked about in the Foreword, you will continue to make Client acquisition a priority. If you don't, you will end up riding the ups and downs of reactionary sales because you are relying on the Random Hope Strategy of Business. I did that for much too long in my early businesses.

Block schedule your very few, very important priorities, and do everything else in the white spaces of life.

How to Make an Appointment

Making Connection and Conversation appointments are the two highest priorities for anyone who wants to grow their business. And filling those block-scheduled appointment holes is an art form. I've seen the following kind of sloppy appointment-making way too often (and I've done it myself):

"Hey, we should get together sometime." "Yes, we should."

Two weeks later: "Do you have time to meet next month?" "Yes."

A week after that: "Hey, toss me a day that might work for you." "November 1st?"

Response the next day: "Great, what time?" "2 p.m.?"

Response the following day: "Great, where would you like to meet?" "Tina's Coffee Shop?"

Response the day after that: "OK, great, see you there."

Nearly a month after the initial contact, two people actually get something on the schedule—and it's usually another two to four weeks out. There's so much wrong with that process.

Over the years, we have experimented with a lot of appointment-making approaches to find what works best to connect with small business owners or individuals in larger companies. For the 13 years I worked with big corporations as my Customers, it sometimes required a different approach because many of those appointments included coordinating multiple people's schedules. But generally, we found the following system worked extremely efficiently, including with individuals in giant corporations.

Assume today is Monday, October 16:

"Miranda, I'd love to connect with you on either Wednesday, November 1, at 11 a.m., or Thursday, November 9, at 2 p.m. I'll suggest Tina's Coffee Shop as a starter. And if either of those dates or that location doesn't work, let me know what might and I'll see if I can make that work."

What happened as your potential Client or Lumberjack heard the above voicemail or read your text is similar to what happens in slow motion with the referral question from Chapter 8 ("Do you know one other person who might benefit from the experience you're having?") When you use the above scheduling approach, they consciously (or, more likely, unconsciously) hear something like:

- They are taking charge and *leading*, not in a controlling way but in a helpful, "giving me options" way. If our relationship is starting with this kind of clarity and flexibility, they are likely to be this helpful going forward as well. This will probably be a low-maintenance relationship where they suggest and I respond. (Insert "sigh of relief" emoji here.)
- They're not pushy or in a sales panic. They don't need to meet for at least a couple of weeks, which is great. I'm not dealing with someone who needs money *now* and wants to separate me from some of mine.
- They're totally open to me taking the lead if I want to. Again, not a control freak—just helpful. Nice.

There are some other things going on here as well that Miranda may not pick up on. There are four basic elements of this invitation— simple, but very intentional:

1. **Two Invitations**. Give them two possibilities to choose from, using the following criteria.
2. **Two Different Days of the Week**. Some people are always very busy on a specific day of the week, like Wednesdays, and open on another. This makes it more likely you'll hit one of their open days.
3. **Morning and Afternoon**. Some people are in the office every morning and meet with people in the afternoons, while others might do the opposite. Giving both a morning and an afternoon option increases your chances of getting a positive response.

4. **Two and Three Weeks Out**. Most people are dragged along by the Tyranny of the Urgent because they are married to the Random Hope Strategy of Business. As a result, many people will have filled their schedules for this week and next. They will have some pretty good openings two weeks out because other Random Hopers haven't put much on their schedules yet, and they will be largely wide open three weeks out. But four weeks is more than their short-term decision-making mindset can handle.

If you consistently invite people to meet with you two to three weeks from now, you are much more likely to get them on your schedule. And you will always have a full schedule in the coming week because you planned ahead, instead of scrambling to make something happen at the last minute.

Once you settle on a date, time, and place, one more way to demonstrate your leadership is to send them a calendar invite so they don't have to mess with that, either. Lead from the start. It's a great way to build their trust and confidence in you right away.

I also recommend that you text or leave them a voicemail (I prefer voicemail—it's closer to a hug. And who knows? They might actually pick up), and then email them as well. The text or voicemail should be short and point to the email: "Hi, Tom. Sarah said we should connect. It seems I might have Customers you might want, and if that's true, I'm guessing you might also know people who could be a fit for us. I'd love to get together and see if we could push each other forward. I sent an email (or text) with a couple of suggested times so you can just click and respond. I really look forward to meeting you."

Then the text or email would say something like this: "Tom, Sarah mentioned we should connect, and I'd love to do that. I can meet either next Wednesday at 2 p.m., or two weeks out on Tuesday at 10:30 a.m. at Tina's Coffee Shop. If neither of those work, please suggest a day and time. I look forward to meeting you."

There are multiple advantages to this approach. First, you've connected with them twice already (voicemail/text and email). This Recency and Frequency is a good start. Second, you took charge and suggested dates, times, and places, but you also gave them the option of suggesting something else. This "actionable" communication from you tells them you will lead and make it easy for them to respond, but you're also not dictating.

As an important aside, propose coffee, not breakfast or lunch. With rare exceptions, lunch adds no value to the meeting, costs more money (you invited, so you're buying), and takes more time than you need to have a great Conversation. And if either of you feel the meeting is clearly not going anywhere, coffee can end a lot faster.

Don't shy away from block scheduling or from being very specific and intentional about getting an appointment. Run toward these tools, embrace whichever aspects will help you double your income, and join the few disciplined business owners and Independent Agents who succeed because they are intentional.

My Next One Thing: Block Scheduling and Making an Appointment

How can you apply block scheduling to your sales and marketing efforts? Be specific.

Is there anything in the way you make appointments that needs to be revised or improved? Be specific.

What is your Blinding Flash of the Obvious from this chapter, and how will you apply it?

_____

Who will you share your Next One Thing with? _____

_____ When? _____

Afterword:

DO YOU WANT IT BAD ENOUGH?

For my 30th birthday, I gave myself the present of running a marathon. Some self-gifts are better than others.

Friends of mine had run this marathon the year before, so of course it seemed to make sense that I should do it, too. I had never run more than two and a half miles, a couple of times a week, and it was only 21 weeks to the starting horn. But that just seemed to make it more appealing. You know: chase tough, audacious goals, and all that.

I found a book on how to run a marathon, set up a daily training schedule based on how many weeks I had to prepare, bought some new shoes (which still had no cushion; I might as well have run in sandals), and took off. After a few weeks, I was up to three to five miles a day, with one longer run that got longer each week of training. And each week I was running more miles. The main lesson I was learning was that if I didn't get my run in early, I would find myself out at 10 p.m. to stay on schedule.

My wife, Diane, had been running for years, long before I had ever met her. She ran two to three miles, five to six days a week. At the beginning of my training, I could follow—or, more accurately, lag behind—her for my run. Soon I could run with her, and then I would keep going when she finished. I pressed on, stayed disciplined, finished the marathon, sat under a tree and cried from mental and emotional exhaustion, checked the marathon off my list, and quickly went back to running a couple of miles once or twice a week. Diane went on to run two to three miles a day for three more decades before her knees got in her way, and then she switched to other faithful daily exercises.

The Tortoise and the Hare

Which of us got the most out of running? Clearly, Diane did. I saw my goal of running the marathon the way the hare did—putting on a brief, temporary burst of speed. Diane was the tortoise, always putting one foot in front of the other, taking the long view of how running could help her. And it's the tortoise, who moves relentlessly and resolutely forward, who always wins. I learned a valuable life lesson from my marathon, which, as always for me, translated into a business lesson. I learned the important difference between discipline and diligence, why you need both, and why it matters in sales.

The Value of Discipline

I was very disciplined during the five and a half months I spent training for the marathon. I don't think I missed more than a day or two of training. I did it all by the book and beat my desired time by more than 15 minutes. Discipline is very effective for meeting short-term goals. We can see clearly what needs to be done in the short term, do it, and see tangible, near-term results. If you take the 90-Day, Double Your Income Challenge we've presented in this book, and you are disciplined and focused on your First Domino, you are very likely to get what you intend. Congratulations—but that's just the beginning.

While you read this book, you left your analog world of endless combinations of possible sales tactics that usually just result in

Playing Office. And you entered the clarity of the digital world, which only has two options: "Will I execute on my First Domino today? Yes = one, and No = zero."

Discipline is about saying one small, simple "yes" right now. We stack small "right now" yeses to build a successful business and, more important, a fulfilled life. Whenever I don't feel like saying "yes," I immediately review my sales and business goals in light of my Big Why—those few Lifetime Goals that put business in its proper context and make it all worthwhile.[27] It's less often about "not feeling like it today" and more about "What am I stacking here? Forward progress or stagnation?" My Big Why helps me stay disciplined and get back on the horse when I fall off.

One of the joys of business discipline, combined with tracking our numbers, is that we get to see progress every day. In sales, and in life, we should commit to the following discipline:

Use today to build tomorrow.

Stack disciplined thoughts, feelings, and actions all week, keep building on that for years, and you will "reap what you sow" for a lifetime. But to build something lasting, we need something deeper than the discipline to run a race once; we need the diligence of the tortoise: plodding along ceaselessly, doing the few simple and sometimes difficult things that will grow our business best as we stack one day on the next.

---

27 For more on what we call the Big Why and on Lifetime Goals, connect with us at www.3to5Club.com/resources.

The Deeper Value of Diligence

A bricklayer came home after a hard day,[28] and his spouse asked how his day went. He replied, "Oh, OK, I guess, we laid bricks all day, so nothing special." His coworker got home, and his spouse asked how his day went. "Pretty good, thanks, we're building a wall, and it looked like we made a lot of progress today." A third spouse asked the same question, and the third bricklayer replied, "I had a great day—we're building a cathedral. If we each lay 1,000 bricks every day, we'll be done in 46 more months. Today we all averaged 1,120 bricks each. At that pace, this amazing structure will be done in 39 months. I can't wait to get back at it again tomorrow and see how we do. Just 38 months and 29 days to go." There is a big difference between stacking bricks for a day and building a cathedral based on written metrics.

Discipline helped me prepare for a one-time challenge of building a small wall. Diligence kept Diane running regularly for many decades, building her cathedral of fitness and health. I was a short-lived flash in the pan. She won the race by thousands of miles, and she did it with diligence. The long view is always the best one. It allows us to look past today's rain and clouds and see the future harvest. It helps us learn to plod forward instead of wrecking ourselves on the shores of hyperactive quarterly or yearly massive sales attacks that just estrange us from potential Customers.

Remember *conation*. It is a combination of short-term discipline (I want something so badly that I'm already doing it) and long-term diligence (the will to succeed that manifests itself in single-minded pursuit of a goal). And remember *velleity*, which causes us to Play Office: the true desire, *with no real intention of doing anything*. Conation is intuition in action, and it is the embodiment of both discipline and diligence.

---

28 Thanks again to Art Radtke for sharing the bones of this story with me many years ago.

As you develop the digital world of your First Domino, keep in mind that the Rugged Individualist is dead. Power is not found in self-sufficiency but in vulnerability and transparency. It took me many decades to learn that. I encourage you to get a Support Partner who will come alongside you on a weekly basis to share all your victories and help defeat impostors—and then help you turn them into fascinating seminars. Even better, get them to join you in doubling their revenue or income, or some other "I dare you" 90-day goal. And then support each other for those 90 days of discipline and a lifetime of trudging, relentless diligence.

Make More Money in Less Time

I'm rabid and relentless about figuring out how to make more money in less time. Income Producers make more money in *more* time. Business owners figure out how to make more money in *less* time. Most people who think they are Business owners are actually Income Producers. They own a job, not a company, and are hostages of their own creation. See my book *Making Money Is Killing Your Business* to see how I learned to make more money in less time, get off the business treadmill, and have Freedom *in* my business, not *from* it.

Every principle, practice, and tool in this book can help you make more money in less time. As you move on these things, notice which ones energize you and which ones drain you, and then delegate to others the things that slow your roll. According to the book *Thrive: How Realtors can Succeed in a Down Market,* people who are selling, whether they are business owners or Independent Agents, make up to 310 percent more than the average by simply learning to do the things that energize them and farming out the rest to virtual assistants or others in their business.[29]

I want you to finish reading this book with conative resolve, define in writing what you want in sales and in life, embrace it, and run toward it with everything you've got until you get it. Commit to the Law of Intention: You get what you intend, not what you hope for.

And be the stream running downhill. The shortest route to the ocean is the path of least resistance, combined with the passion and impatience to never give up on your goal, which means sometimes you run right through the resistance. Remember it's always about the result, and the process will change as the world interacts with your stream. Design your life and relentlessly flow into it.

And finally: serve; don't sell. Take the long view. Devise a plan to serve your potential Customers that you can stick to for years. Then stack one simple digital yes day on top of another and build your tomorrow, one cathedral brick at a time. Perhaps no one will be impressed today, but everybody will be impressed a few years from now. The tortoise *always* wins.

You get what you intend, not what you hope for. Intend to *Sell Less, Earn More*—serve; don't sell.

---

29 For a list of delegation strategies that will help you make more money in less time, in sales as well as in the rest of your business, go to 3to5Club.com/SDS.

FIND OUT MORE

Crankset Group and 3to5 Club Resources

**To access resources below visit
www.3to5club.com/resources**

www.3to5Club.com and www.CranksetGroup.com
Grow@CranksetGroup.com or call us at 303-422-6675
Chuck Blakeman and other
Crankset Group Business Advisors are available for:

Get Off The Treadmill Podcast—a short, weekly podcast specifically
for small business owners by small business owners. A mix of
Chuck's personal business insights and small business owner guests'
experiences. https://podcast.3to5club.com/

One2One Business Advisory with business owners and business leaders.
See above contact information.

Speaking to mastermind groups, associations, and keynotes to thousands.
See above contact information.
- 15 Minute TEDx Sample: https://www.youtube.com/
watch?v=ewA2BqbWhUQ

Workshops and Seminars to owners, leaders, and/or strategic and tactical teams. See above contact information.

Peer Advisory mastermind group participation, which we presently have in person on three continents, and via online groups worldwide; 3to5 Club and 3to5 Board. See above contact information.

FasTrak—Double Your Income in 90 Days. Our business development course on which this book is based, held quarterly in person and via zoom. https://www.3to5club.com/DoubleYourIncome/ or above contact information.

Two-Page Strategic Plan Online—a simple, powerful, self-guided course to doing business planning and learn how to plan strategically on just two pages. Includes live office hours. See https://www.3to5club.com/StrategicPlanCourse/ or above contact information.

Freedom Mapping Online—Self-guided course to get you and everyone in your business into the highest and best use of their time and talents, and create freedom IN your business, not FROM it. See https://www.3to5club.com/FreedomMapping/ or above contact information.

3to5ClubForMe—a self-guided version of our internationally acclaimed 3to5 Club. You will pace yourself using Chuck's videos and handouts, and will have a worldwide community available to grow together in forums and virtually with each other. You will also have access to most of Chuck's workshops and seminars for free. https://www.3to5club.com/ForMe or above contact information.

Webinars—for short, content-rich audio/video enrichment. https://www.3to5club.com/Webinars or above contact information.

Other Resources

https://apexprofile.com/—the only psychometric profile built specifically for business owners. Find out what you're good at and what you should hire or train others to do.

Making Money Is Killing Your Business: How to build a business you love, and get a life, too. Chuck Blakeman's #1 Rated Business Book on how to make MORE money in LESS time, get off the treadmill, and get back to the passion that brought you into business in the first place. https://bit.ly/3ZCTapR

Re-Humanizing The Workplace by Giving Everybody Their Brain Back. Chuck Blakeman's Top Ten business book on how to build a Participation Age company with Distributed Decision-Making that creates 100 percent engagement and eliminates the management tax, the hiring/attrition tax, and the training tax. https://bit.ly/4dVNxY5

> **Access the resources listed above by visiting www.3to5club.com/resources**

INDEX